And Breathe

Rebecca Dennis is the founder of www.breathingtree.co.uk and a qualified breath coach and workshop leader. She lived with depression for nearly 20 years before discovering Transformational Breath, which she has studied with founder Judith Kravitz in Mexico and Miami and other influential trainers in Italy and in the UK. Her clients come with many different issues including stress, anxiety, addiction, abuse, depression, ME, respiratory problems, trauma, sleeping patterns, focus, lack of energy, physical problems and low self-esteem. Conscious breathwork continues to show her it is the ultimate key to our wellbeing, health and inner peace.

And Breathe

Rebecca Dennis

ORION
SPRING

First published in Great Britain in 2016
by Orion Spring
an imprint of The Orion Publishing Group Ltd
Carmelite House, 50 Victoria Embankment
London EC4Y 0DZ

An Hachette UK Company

1 3 5 7 9 10 8 6 4 2

ISBN (Trade paperback) 978 1 4091 6832 4
ISBN (eBook) 978 1 4091 6833 1

Typeset by Input Data Services Ltd, Bridgwater, Somerset

Printed and bound by CPI Group (UK) Ltd, Croydon, CR0 4YY

www.orionbooks.co.uk

ORION
SPRING

Contents

Introduction

....

Begin by paying attention to your breath.

Even as you read these next few words, be aware of the breath.

Notice that you are breathing and notice the rhythm of your breath.

Realise that it is easy to read and be aware of the breath at the same time.

Notice the rise and fall of your breath.

Pay attention to the inhale and the exhale.

Notice the feelings and sensations of the breath flowing in and out.

Pay close attention to the flow of your breath.

Take in each word.

Are you ready to begin? Let's do it!

....

A little history

The most important thing in life is to breathe – after all, we live to breathe and we breathe to live. We cannot exist without it. The first thing we do when we make our entrance into the world is breathe, and it is the last thing we do when we exit.

A little statistic for you: we inhale and exhale around 20,000 times a day, yet most of us pay little attention to how we breathe or how deeply it affects us. So, why should we notice how we breathe? It's a sad fact that in our increasingly demanding and complex world very few people are aware of the detrimental effects that improper breathing can have on our health and general wellbeing.

We teach our young to walk, communicate, bathe, eat and socialise, yet educating them about the healing power of their breath is not a priority. It's not even on the radar, but trust me, that is about to change. I want to encourage you to be aware of your breath and share the multitude of wonderful benefits that emerge from breathing consciously. How we breathe is indicative of how we feel about life.

Becoming the expert of your breath

One of the reasons I wanted to write this book was to release self-empowerment to you, the reader, and to help you understand its power. Breathing consciously allows us to access all the answers that are inside us. Learning to breathe properly and connecting with our emotions enables our life-force energy to flow and deal with the obstacles and daily challenges that we face.

In short, our breath is our medicine, a powerful tool that all too often we take for granted. I want to take you on this journey into a deeper understanding of our breath and what it can do for us by sharing my experiences, offering handy tips, delving into medical and scientific research, and documenting my clients' stories.

You may think you don't need to be told how to breathe. It's natural, right? We just do it without thinking, don't we? If you think that, this book is *definitely* for you, whether you are a stay-at-home mum, a student studying for your exams or a jet-setting CEO. I can't wait for you to experience the remarkable benefits of practising healthy breathing.

I'm going to include some simple, easy-to-remember exercises that can be incorporated into your daily life with a minimum of fuss. You don't need an expensive one-to-one session in a state-of-the-art yoga studio; you can do most of these exercises anywhere – on the tube, at your desk, standing in the supermarket queue, walking the dog, even in the bathroom!

These short, simple exercises are derived from everything I have learned from my teachings with some truly inspirational instructors. Once you get a routine going and a regular practice, these exercises will help you sleep, calm your nerves and leave you feeling inspired, energised and focused. Sounds like a miracle, right? Well, certainly in my eyes, it is!

When I first told friends I was teaching breathwork they would look confused, or would laugh at the thought of making a living from showing people how to breathe. If I had a pound for every time I heard 'But we all breathe naturally, so why do we need to be taught how to do it?' I'd be writing this from my beach house in Mexico (sadly I'm not). It sounds almost too simple, but hear me when I tell you that the majority of teenagers and adults have lost their natural ability to breathe fully. As a result of this, we slowly begin to shut down parts of ourselves. We are conditioned from an early age to control our feelings. Think about how we hold our breath when unwanted emotions bubble to the surface: our muscle tissues contract and our breath becomes restricted as we hold on to old conditioning patterns of behaviour. Our body has a biological recording of our past with each breath.

It's called 'transformational' for a reason

The results I see from teaching breathwork are always so powerful they blow me away. I have no idea what is going to happen in a session. Each one is unique. I feel very blessed to have witnessed amazing transformations in the lives of the people I teach.

For example, one CEO came to me because he'd started experiencing frightening panic attacks and could no longer attend board meetings or give presentations. Through our breathwork he came to understand what he was subconsciously holding on to, and the panic attacks ceased.

Another client had been trying to get pregnant for 10 years. After a few breath sessions, she fell pregnant with her first child. I also teach a young lady whose anxiety was so extreme that she couldn't leave the house. Connecting to her breath has helped her to manage the condition and she has regained control of her life.

A boxer who was holding on to anger that stemmed from

his unhappy childhood learned to let go during his fifth session with me, and now channels his energy in a positive way into his career. A woman in an unhappy marriage was about to leave her husband until breathing sessions helped her realise it was her past that was preventing her from being happy in her marriage.

A war veteran finally let go of the hurt and trauma she had been holding on to from her time in Afghanistan, while an insomniac client who would go for weeks on end without sleep conquered that demon. All these life-changing stories (we'll hear more about them later) are a result of breathwork. This therapy is unique because there are parts of ourselves we can't necessarily access through talk therapy, but the breath can get us there, if we allow it to.

When I first came across breathwork, I couldn't understand why everyone wasn't doing it. In my opinion, it is the most powerful, accessible and transformative tool we have.

Breathwork not only changed my life, it saved my life

I have lived with depression for over 20 years, 15 of which were spent on prescribed medication. I self-medicated too, with alcohol and recreational drugs, and reached a point in my 30s where I knew I needed help but didn't know how to get it.

The black dog of depression jumped on my back when I was in my teens. Back in the 1980s, depression was somewhat taboo, and people chose not to discuss it as there was a real stigma attached. I used to watch people going about their everyday life and wonder if they felt as bad as I did. Did everyone feel distanced from the flow of life and have this awkward disconnection from their body, or was it just me?

At my lowest point, I felt that life was no longer worth living. I limped on with chronic emotional depression and a real sense of complete physical depletion. My energy levels were so low that often I would barely move my limbs. On these days, I was just existing, watching the clock and wishing the day away. I had no sense of living in a healthy, vital way. I would regularly have dark suicidal thoughts and spent hours planning different ways to exit the world.

Unable to share these irrational thoughts (like many depressed people, I didn't want to burden others), I would hide away, avoiding contact, feeling numb, disconnected and in despair at not being able to shift my mood. There is so much shame around depression, so it often goes unseen. If you are depressed, it's not obvious to other people that you are unwell – you don't have a plaster cast or a bandage.

Two months before I discovered Transformational Breath®, I attempted to take my own life, ingesting a combination of alcohol and pills. Fortunately for me, that night there were some Earth angels – my best friends Jamie and Louisa – who called at the right time. My sister Sarah took me to hospital in an ambulance.

I went home the following day, and that week I found a therapist who specialised in cognitive behavioural therapy.

The support from my sister, my mum and my closest friends is what got me through. I only told a handful of people what had happened, because I was ashamed. Taking your own life is one of the most selfish acts you can commit, but I know what it's like to be in that moment, feeling it would be better for everyone if you were no longer there.

It's not easy living with or being friends with a person with depression. I've been overwhelmed by shame and self-hatred for so many years. It is draining for those around you, and I am for ever grateful to the wonderful souls who did not give up on me and kept me going when I felt I had nothing left to give. I am here because they loved me.

They loved me with their silence and their kind, non-judgemental words. They loved me with their willingness to be as uncomfortable as I was and sit there with me, or just let me know that they were there for me. Grateful doesn't begin to cover it.

From rock bottom to recovery

After many years working in the crazy world of entertainment and media (where I indulged in a hedonistic 'work hard, play harder' lifestyle), I knew I needed to get out and do something else. I had some incredible experiences making music videos and albums, going to festivals, meeting my idols and touring with musicians.

I also experienced some of the lowest moments of my life during that period. I was a mistress of disguise, a quirky, funny, sociable and outgoing girl with the dream job, at least from the outside looking in. However, the cracks soon began to show.

The medication wasn't really working anymore, and I was finding it increasingly hard to focus and function. I was living in a shared house in London with two friends. I was burnt out and fragile and the depression and anxiety were starting to suck me under.

One day I walked into a courtyard and found a place that immediately felt magical and comforting, almost womb-like. It was the Special Yoga Foundation in north-west London, run by an inspiring lady called Jo Manuel, where children with special needs practise yoga and classes are accessible to everyone. It offers families from all walks of life this wonderful therapy that helps children with movement and breath. I immediately fell in love with the place.

Watching a teacher take an unsettled child for a lesson and then seeing the child emerge relaxed, calm and smiling put things into perspective for me. It reminded me of being back in India, where I had lived for six months, where the pace was gentle and *shanti*. It was just what I needed. I began working part-time on reception, and was soon offered a job running their fundraising and events programme.

It was here that I encountered a major influence in my life: my yoga instructor Francis D'Angelo. He used humour in his class to help us let go of any judgement about how good we were, and shared little pearls of wisdom using words that sang to my soul.

One day, in one of the first classes I attended with Francis, I just could not switch off. I was constantly looking at the clock, thinking about all the jobs I should have been doing. I made a feeble excuse and left the class. Francis came running out after me, stopped me from leaving, and told me: 'If anyone needs to be doing this right now, it's you. Come back inside.'

He was right. Putting myself through this practice of self-discovery and healing meant I had to sit with myself, and that was often incredibly uncomfortable. I was constantly trying to run away from myself, but Francis was putting a stop to that. I went back in and I never left another yoga class early.

My introduction to Transformational Breath

The first time I walked into a breath workshop, I did not know what to expect. It was held by a man called Alan Dolan, who went on to become my mentor, during my training, and my friend. His explanation of the work was so clear, and when I started my journey, it was the most dynamic and mind-blowing experience.

I'll try and describe that first amazing session to you (although words can't really do it justice). I could feel every cell in my body releasing and letting go. Physically, mentally and emotionally, I was in a complete state of flux. I was crying and sweating and my whole body was reverberating and vibrating. It was INTENSE! I had no control and totally surrendered to the maelstrom of emotions and physical reactions. It was like being caught in a whirlpool and to struggle was useless.

Afterwards, I felt lighter and, for the first time in a very long time, I was full of hope. I also noticed I could make decisions more clearly and felt really positive. I wanted more.

I realised I had been introduced to something very special and I wasn't going to let it disappear from my life. I needed this.

I want to stress that none of this happened overnight. I used the breath technique I had been taught every day and worked closely with my doctor. Sometimes I'd have dark episodes and wonder if I should go back on medication, but I never did. I began to love myself for the first time and started looking after the body I had been punishing for so long.

I found myself meeting some of the most inspiring people I've ever had the good fortune to come across. I can't help wondering whether I embraced these people because of the state of mind I was now in.

I began to feel whole, complete and physically present. My mind was clear and my emotions were more balanced. After years of suffering anxiety, panic attacks and chronic depression, I was getting to grips with the healing power of my own inner breath.

They say what doesn't kill you makes you stronger – it's true. For the first time, I was able to see 'my story' from a completely different perspective. It made me grateful for the dark times, the hard lessons learned, and the gifts from life and my teachers. My experiences have furnished me with an understanding and empathy for others, and my daily reward is observing similar transformations with my clients by using breathwork.

I also realised for the first time that I and I alone was responsible for my happiness. The only person with the power to let go of the past and stop holding myself back was me. The answer was right under my nose, and I'm proud to tell you I chose life.

Why breathing?

I've always been fascinated by the human body and how it works. I completed a 2-year course in massage and anatomy and set up a small practice as a body-worker. Teaching Transformational Breath myself was my next challenge. I'd explored courses in yoga, energy work and Reiki, but the drive to learn this was like nothing I had experienced before.

What I love about this work is that it is self-healing. As my dear friend Russell says: 'It's a conscious choice by an individual to partake in the practice. No one can breathe for you, which explains why a breathwork practitioner can only ever facilitate an individual – the ultimate choice always remains with the breather.'

Generally, I recommend 3 to 5 sessions with a breathworker: you have all the tools you need to empower yourself in your own self-practice.

There are many teachers in this field, and the key is to find the right one for you. There are sure to be breathing teachers in your area who hold group sessions or one-to-one lessons.

From Mexico . . . with love

I saved enough to book a ticket to Mexico to train with Judith Kravitz, co-founder of the Transformational Breath Foundation. I was three months pregnant, and that week was yet another life-changing experience for me.

Judith was (and is) dynamic, funny, a mother of eight; she taught with such humility, and her energy knew no bounds. She has incredible knowledge based on four decades of developing her conscious breathwork, and wants to share this with the world.

Watching her reading the breath patterns of individuals at first sight and working with them for just a few minutes was enough to see she was passionate and completely instinctive when it came to reading people.

This work is powerful, physical and cathartic, and as I watched her working, I noticed that everyone felt safe and nurtured in her hands. She was not going to qualify anyone until she felt the same about us. Unusually for me, I trusted her from the first moment I met her.

The sessions were very intense as I was releasing old habits and trauma through my breath, but I knew I was in a safe place and that this process was going to be great for me.

Every day of this magical week was a revelation, with layers and layers of my psyche being integrated and released with the help of amazing teachers from all over the world. To cap it all, we could see whales teaching their young how to breach in the sea from our training room.

It felt like new beginnings for the 40 other people on the

course, who were by my side from all walks of life, breathing together and learning this transformative technique as one.

Does anyone actually enjoy public speaking?

I'm sure I'm not alone in detesting the idea of putting myself in front of an audience. In the past, I'd have panic attacks and would resort to a few drinks for Dutch courage, or simply make an excuse and hide.

Letting go of negative patterns of behaviour and learning to be comfortable with who I am and with being seen was a new journey for me. Once you start digging, you don't really stop. It is warrior work and naturally, it can be uncomfortable seeing all the parts of ourselves that we don't necessarily like, upfront and in glorious technicolour.

Learning to love and accept every facet of ourselves, good or bad, is the ultimate goal, so we can feel comfortable in our own skin and truly understand the essence of who we are.

This powerful breathing technique gave me my life back. I was able to reconnect to my feelings and discover what my body and mind needed to feel happy and at peace with the world once again.

The benefits of breathwork

Mental and emotional

Creates space for clarity and a relaxed mind
Feel more centred, calm and balanced

Reduces stress and anxiety
Relieves depression and negative thought patterns
Helps alleviate addictions and eating disorders
Helps sleep patterns
Boosts self-esteem
Feel more positive and energised
Let go of emotional baggage
Release unhealthy patterns, belief systems, past hurts
Let go of repressed and suppressed emotions
Clears past traumas and experiences

Physical

Increases energy
Detoxification
Improves metabolism and helps digestive problems such as IBS and constipation
Relieves muscle tension
Improves wellbeing for many conditions and ailments, such as respiratory issues, asthma, ME, headaches, sleeplessness, low energy – the list is endless!

Spiritual

Expands our inner awareness
Creates feelings of peace
Deepens connection with self and inner wisdom
Deepens creative and sensual energies
Deepens yoga and meditation practice

So why this book?

I am not a master of science, metaphysics or psychotherapy. I'm not a guru. I was just a regular 30-something woman who often found herself in a dark place and did not know how to function or fit in. When I reached the point of hopelessness, I was given the gift of remembering to connect to my breath.

It's important to know that this work is not about learning new tricks; it's about accessing what is buried in our subconscious so we can better understand ourselves. Remembering how to listen to the innate intelligence of our bodies is crucial.

I have met some incredible healers and teachers who have shared their wisdom and knowledge and helped me to understand and evolve my practice. I have met some courageous people who have trusted me with their stories. Seeing the change in these brave beings from breathwork is such a gift.

This book is for all the little voices inside us that have not been heard because they have been silenced or told they are not good enough. It is also for the souls who feel that something is missing but cannot quite determine what it is. Above all, it is about our journey towards reconnecting with our souls through breathwork and learning to trust ourselves, to allow the light back in and to embrace rather than fear our shadow sides.

I hope you enjoy the journey that is about to begin.

As a lover of Forrest Yoga, I had to ask certified Forrest Yoga teacher Kristi Mae Rodelli to contribute to this book. The style of yoga she teaches resonates and speaks to my body. I learnt so much about breath and our bodies by reading the book *Fierce Medicine* by Ana Forrest, and then, thanks to a beautiful coincidence, Kristi was teaching at the place where I practise and see clients. I remember crying silently in my first Forrest Yoga lesson, not in pain but in relief. I was able to let go of tension I had been holding on to for years as I moved through a deep release in my hips. Whenever I can get to Kristi's classes I am there . . .

Kristi Mae Rodelli is a certified Forrest Yoga teacher.

Breathing is something I learned through my yoga practice, but it took a few years and a few teachers before I was taught how to breathe deeply and fully. It really changed my yoga practice and the way I feel when I teach, as well as the way I communicate and live my life.

Using a deep breath when I practise yoga helps me to work struggle-free. I now have a lot more ease in my practice and flexibility in my body. I am less reactive towards exercises or feelings that are challenging or confronting, and relax into the experience of the practice, rather than trying to control it or fight against it.

Breathing releases a lot of tension. If we are tense, angry, scared or stressed, our breathing gets shallow. The muscles tighten and the body gets rigid, creating more tension and stress. When we breathe deeply, we oxygenate the cells and help the growth of muscle in our bodies. When we feel pain or discomfort, we also tend to hold or restrict our breath. Breathing deeply reduces the intensity of pain and minimises feelings of discomfort.

Making my breath a priority has made me stronger and more energised. I no longer get burnt out running around the city teaching classes. Taking in deep inhales is a way to take in energy and feed myself, so when I exhale, I can speak and move from a place that is full, grounded and alive.

Breathing deeply also boosts energy levels, increases stamina, and strengthens and tones our abdominal muscles. Strong abdominals provide a huge amount of support and stability for the spine.

Connecting deeply to my breath has brought more awareness to where I am on all levels. It is not always easy to sink into a place of feeling, because the truths about what we feel can be confronting and uncomfortable. The insights I have gained and continue to gain from connecting to breath help me live a life that supports, energises and inspires me.

When we become curious about the places in our body that are tight or tense and then breathe into them, we can gain a lot of clarity and insight. This process can then become an exploration and an effective tool for clearing uneasy feelings from the body to create the space we need to bring in a quality of energy we wish to have living in our cell tissue.

A simple breathing exercise that I use on a regular basis is Sivananda's pranayama. It relaxes the muscles, establishes rhythm, calms the mind, promotes circulation, and creates a sense of peace. It's an effective way to ground myself, calm my mind, and check how I am feeling at the start of the day. It works beautifully with my students, helping to centre them, bringing enough physical and mental stillness to clarify their intentions, and encourages a deeper, more mindful breath before moving into the more physical part of the yoga practice.

Like any practice, the most challenging part of this exercise is just sitting down to do it. Start small and simple with five rounds of Sivananda's pranayama. As it gets easier to sit for longer, add a few more rounds and begin to make your breath broader and more expansive. Notice where you feel more space, more length and more strength, and acknowledge where you feel more energy and aliveness.

⊱— EXERCISE —⊰

SIVANANDA YOGA EXERCISE FROM KRISTI MAE RODELLI

Sit comfortably in an upright position.

Close your eyes.

Draw in a very slow, long inhale through both nostrils for as long as is comfortable.

Hold the breath for as long as is comfortable.

Exhale through both nostrils for as long as is comfortable.

Repeat five rounds of this exercise and then pause and observe how you feel.

The inhale and exhale don't need to be a particular length, nor do you need to observe the ratio between the inhale and exhale. Make sure that the inhale and exhale are deep and full and practised, without struggle.

In the moment when you are holding the breath, consciously relax your jaw, throat, neck, shoulders, diaphragm and abdominal muscles. The more relaxed you are, the easier it will be to hold the breath for longer.

This exercise can be done seated, or lying down in bed

in the morning to wake yourself up, make yourself more alert, and connect to how you're feeling at the beginning of the day. You can also practise this exercise at work or while studying, to recharge and find fresh energy, or to help you sleep.

**Russell, 35, is a breathworker.
This is his story.**

If I were to sum up in one word what breathwork means to me, it would be 'hope'.

I often joke in workshops that some people feel called to this work and walk willingly into the light, often having stories of miraculous insight and healing which have fuelled a deep knowing that it is their path to share it with the world.

Then there are others who pretend they don't hear the call, only to get dragged kicking and screaming backwards through the same door by life circumstances.

You might guess which category I fall into, but in truth I didn't go down without a fight. I've learned that life gives us the challenges we need to face our fears. Always. Our current circumstances are exactly what we need in order to grow.

Life brought me to my knees in January 2010. I had successfully climbed the corporate ladder working at an international bank, and had just taken the plunge, purchasing a property with my then partner. But at a time that should have been the happiest of my life, getting ready to build a future and maybe even start a family, things were falling apart.

My moment of clarity came in our beautiful Edinburgh flat one Saturday morning. My partner, who had been battling severe depression for some time, was still asleep (her preference for slumber over my company was one of the most noticeable symptoms of her ongoing inner struggle).

I felt alone, frustrated, helpless and powerless. I had a mortgage I was solely responsible for, a job that was slowly killing me, my energy levels were at rock bottom, and I was stuck in a sedentary and unhealthy lifestyle.

I felt absolutely trapped with no idea what to do next. At that moment I asked for help. The answer was very clear.

Breathe. Conscious breathing.

I googled 'conscious breathing' and came across a series of YouTube videos about Transformational Breath. The co-founder, Judith Kravitz, had me hooked when she stated: 'Full mental health is possible.'

Coming from a family where mental health issues were familiar territory, along with alcoholism, depression, epilepsy, schizophrenia and anxiety, it was not a promise that I took lightly. But losing the woman I loved to a condition I didn't understand, and knowing in my heart that I was rapidly following suit, I knew I needed to learn more.

I booked myself a breath session and life has not been the same since. I believe our outside circumstances are a mirror to what is going on inside us. The two are inextricably linked.

My life changed, but I won't sugarcoat it. A lot of it was messy and painful. It required wading knee-deep into stuff I would have rather not faced, but my breath guided me through. It continues to fuel my love affair with personal growth and healing while presenting challenges that help me mature and evolve. It also gives me hope, not just for me, but for our world.

The death of my dad last year was a harsh reminder that this life of ours is precious. Breath gave me the awareness to live every moment, be it painful, healing, mystical or joyful. Processing my grief needed time, space and the love and support from my family and friends.

Breath has simply accelerated the process, helping to transform personal pain into empathy, compassion, gratitude and, ultimately, love.

In a world of hype and quick fixes, breath is real. It is life, not just the good stuff but the messy bits too, the uncomfortable truths and the bits we sometimes wish weren't there.

Each breath reminds me that we are intrinsically linked to the world around us. We are all in this together, breathing the same air. It is the fundamental exchange of gases that connects us to the world around us.

Transformational Breath has opened my life to change, growth, spirituality and other possibilities that I could never have imagined. In real terms, I have lost a significant amount of weight, improved my exercise and dietary habits, and feel clear, calm and connected.

We can only breathe now. Not yesterday, not tomorrow. Anything can be transformed and our breath can guide us there.

Breath Awareness

What is breath awareness?

As we continue through this book, you'll be asked in some exercises to be aware of your breath. This simply means being present and noticing what your breathing is like, whether it's shallow, long, flowing, short, easy, controlled or laboured.

Little children teach us to be present. Think of a child, happy and content, playing in their imagination, free of inhibitions. They are in the moment, not flitting from thought to thought. They aren't thinking, 'What if this or that happens?' or 'I wonder what I am going to do with my life.' Somewhere along the line, we lose that.

Children sense when an adult isn't being present. My son regularly catches me out when my thoughts are straying, and will literally hold my head and turn it towards him to get my attention!

In everyday moments, it's useful to come back and be aware of your breath. Think about times when you are finding it hard to focus in a meeting, or you are blocked while writing an email, in a challenging conversation or studying for a difficult exam. At times like these, we tend to drift off or get distracted, so focusing on the breath brings us back to being present.

There is rarely a time when life is simple, but instead of fighting that, we should view every moment as a chance to let go, take a breath, allow a pause between your inhale and your exhale, and concentrate on the art of simply being.

We are so busy trying to get to the next place, worrying we'll run out of time, that we forget to acknowledge the pause, where we are right now in the present moment. Focusing on the pause helps us to be here in the now and not in the future or the past. The world will not stop spinning if we pause and take a deep breath.

Conscious breathing can also help to cleanse us of toxins that have built up in the body and the mind. Our body has an innate wisdom, and when we connect to it, we can receive useful insights that dispel the clutter. It helps rid us of worries and tensions and brings us back to our true nature and the essence of who we are. We just have to let it do its work!

Let's start with a simple exercise.

⊨ EXERCISE ⊨

DON'T JUDGE YOUR BREATH, JUST ACCEPT WHERE IT IS TODAY

Close your eyes and take a moment, then inhale through your nose and release the exhale through your mouth.

Notice how the breath feels as it comes through your nose and out of your mouth.

Keep practising this four or five times, and rather than being the breather, become the observer.

Take note of how your body feels. Is it relaxed or does it feel tense?

Can you feel any tightness or restriction?

Is the breath flowing in and out?

What muscles do you notice working as you breathe?

Is it easier to inhale or exhale?

There is no right or wrong, this is just an exercise for you to become aware of your breath and your first step towards understanding how you breathe.

The power of breath

The breath is more powerful than you may think. I witness its magic every day with clients and through my own experiences. Connecting to your breath brings you to the spirit of who you are, taking you inwards on a dance with your internal wisdom and awareness. It's the gateway to our inner world and an indicator of our general state of being.

It's also our very life force, but the fact is we take our breath for granted. Every breath we take profoundly influences our health and happiness on countless levels. Your breath is waiting patiently for you to connect to it. It wants you to hear the messages that it has for you.

Are you ready to begin? You may as well start now, as there is no good or bad time. There is only now. There will be many excuses along the way to not practise the exercises in this book. Trust me, I've heard them all.

'*There is not enough time.*' Try just 5 minutes a day; I promise it will make your day more productive.

'*I'll start tomorrow.*' What's wrong with today?

'*Nothing's happening.*' I beg to differ; something is ALWAYS happening, even if you aren't feeling it.

Notice resistance; it's a great flag, so breathe through it and be aware of how you come out the other side.

Breathwork is a bit like taking your breath to the gym. In the same way that we take our car to the garage for an MOT, we are bringing our breath on a journey, clearing, unclogging or unblocking systems that need a little maintenance. Think of it as a reset and recalibration of our body.

How the breath helps every system in the body

Breathing heals on many levels, and understanding how it performs this function is good for our mental and physical wellbeing. Our breath constantly converts our life-sustaining energy, taking in oxygen, invigorating red blood cells and expelling carbon dioxide, which is a metabolic waste product.

By breathing deeply, you allow the diaphragm to drop downwards, the rib cage to expand and create more space for the lungs to inflate. By mastering the art of deep breathing, increased oxygen floods into the body, eventually helping the heart pace to slow down to create feelings of calmness and relaxation.

In this way we create space for creativity and clarity of the mind. The breath is the bridge between our mind and body. We know our physical body can't live without breathing and breath is a reflection on how we live our life. Al Lee and Don Campbell's book *Perfect Breathing: Transform Your Life One Breath at a Time*, from which this section has been adapted, illustrates this perfectly too.

....

If I had to limit my advice on healthier living to just one tip, it would be simply to learn how to breathe correctly.

Dr Andrew Weil, wellness expert

....

In a nutshell . . .

Breath detoxifies, releases toxins and strengthens the immune system

Around 70% of our toxins are released from our body through our breath. Carbon dioxide is a natural waste product of your body's metabolism. Breathing deeply helps the systems in the body to process this more efficiently.

Breath increases energy

Oxygen is the most essential natural resource required by our cells. We can go without food for up to 40 days and without water for 3 days, yet we can die after just a few minutes of not breathing. From a purely physical point of view, breath equals life.

Breath improves the respiratory system

Breathing deeply helps to release tension in the diaphragm and primary breathing muscles, relieving many long-term respiratory issues such as asthma and breathlessness. It opens up the chest, releasing tension from the intercostal muscles and around the scapula, erector spinae and trapezius muscles, allowing for a more relaxed posture.

Breath calms the nervous system

Deep breathing activates the parasympathetic nervous system, bringing us into a relaxed state. It functions in the opposite way to the sympathetic nervous system, which stimulates activities associated with the fight-or-flight response.

Breath strengthens the lymphatic system

The lymphatic system depends on gravity, muscle movement and breathing to keep flowing so that the body can be cleansed. Deep breathing can play an important role in protecting the body from bacteria, viruses and other threats to our health.

Breath releases muscle tension

When we are stressed or experience uncomfortable feelings such as anger or pain, our breath becomes shallow and our muscle tissues contract. Deep breathing helps to release this.

Breath improves the cardiovascular system

Deep diaphragmatic breathing tones, massages and increases circulation to the heart, liver, brain and reproductive organs. In one study of heart attack patients, 100% of the patients were chest breathers whose breathing involved very little diaphragm or belly expansion. Another study found that patients who survived a heart attack and who adopted an exercise regime and breath training afterwards experienced a 50% reduction in their risk factor of another heart attack over the following 5 years.

Breath elevates the digestive system

Deeper breathing results in an increased blood flow in the digestive tract, which encourages intestinal action and improves overall digestion, alleviating irritable bowel syndrome and constipation. In addition, deeper breathing results in a calmer nervous system which in turn enhances optimum digestion.

Breath affects our mental state

The quality of our breath helps to relax the mind and enhance the ability to learn, focus, concentrate and memorise. The brain requires a great deal of oxygen to function and increased intake of oxygen helps us to achieve clarity and feel grounded and productive. It also relieves stress, anxiety, depression and negative thought patterns. Breathing properly can help us overcome addictive patterns of behaviour and eating disorders, as well as igniting creativity and passion.

Breath keeps us looking youthful

It's a universal truth that a happy face is more beautiful than a stressed or angry one. Even better news: breathing deeply slows the ageing process by increasing secretion of anti-ageing hormones! By reducing stress, it improves our mood, elevating the levels of serotonin and endorphins. *The Telomere Effect* by Dr Elizabeth Blackburn and Dr Elissa Epel (to be published January 2017) chronicles a 2013 study by Harvard Medical School's psychiatry department, which discovered that people who meditate daily for four years have longer telomeres – the protective caps found on the end of chromosomes – than those who do not. Short telomeres have been linked to premature cellular ageing.

Is there anything the breath cannot do?

In a word, no. Good breathing helps us feel more confident and able to let go of old belief systems and negative thought patterns that no longer serve us. Releasing old stories and past dramas previously held on to on a subconscious level gives us new emotional depth. By expanding our awareness inside, breathing has a spiritual effect too, deepening yoga and meditation practice, creating inner peace, and leading us to higher states of consciousness. As if that isn't enough, it can also reinvigorate sexual energy, deepen creative expression, improve sleep patterns and lower blood pressure.

Judith Kravitz sums it up thus:

> The breath holds the key to healing our mental health because we can consciously change our chemistry as well as our

attitude by changing the depth, rhythm and rate of our breathing. As we make these changes, our perspectives and attitudes are altered to engage a more positive mind–body state, thereby dramatically improving our sense of wellbeing. Not only does deep conscious breathing improve mental clarity of the physical brain and conscious mind, it also accesses the subconscious mind.

Adjusting breathing patterns

By correcting unhealthy breathing patterns, we can fully access our respiratory system, letting go of unwanted emotional blockages or trauma being held on to in the body.

Our breath patterns are unique, like a thumbprint, and show how we operate in our daily lives. We are able to read how people relate to themselves and the world as well as how they relate to others. Breathing techniques can be used to help shift patterns that may be preventing us from living to our full potential.

And science agrees

Science recognises that emotions trigger sensations in our body. Butterflies in the tummy or a red face when feeling embarrassed are physical manifestations sparked directly by emotions.

In a study conducted at Aalto University's School of Science in Finland, 700 men and women were shown two silhouettes alongside emotionally charged words, movies, stories or facial expressions. They were asked to mark the bodily regions on the silhouettes where they personally felt a physical response to each emotional image. The body maps revealed that most people had similar physical sensations in response to each emotional state.

Say you see a snake and you feel fear. Your nervous system increases oxygen to your muscles and raises your heart rate so you can deal with the threat. It's an automated system. We don't have to think about it.

Dr Lauri Nummenmaa, Study Leader at Aalto University

The history of breathwork: East vs West

Every culture in the history of the world has in some way acknowledged the existence of a life-force energy within the human body. The intertwined relationship between breath and the state of our health has been recognised for centuries in the medical and meditational practices of the East.

In the West, breathing is seen as a physiological process to supply the body with oxygen, but breathing can be done in more systematic and conscious ways. We should view the breath as a primary vehicle for life energy, a vital link between the mind and the body.

The Indians call it *prana*, the Chinese call it *chi* and the Japanese have dubbed it *ki*. These cultures have used the breath to facilitate health and wellbeing since time immemorial.

Breathwork is divided into modern and ancient techniques. The modern techniques comprise methods such as rebirthing, Holotropic Breathwork™ and Transformational Breath, with many more still evolving. Ancient techniques include pranayama (yoga), chi gong and t'ai chi.

Key figures

Leonard Orr is the grandfather and founder of the breathwork movement. His pioneering work identified the trauma we hold on to, such as birth trauma, parental and peer authority trauma, and unconscious death urge.

According to Leonard Orr: 'The purpose of conscious breathing is not primarily the movement of air but the movement of energy. If you do a relaxed, connected breathing cycle for a few minutes, you will begin to experience dynamic energy flows within your body. These energy flows are the merging of spirit and matter.'

In the 1970s he developed the technique known as 'connected breathing', whereby the inhale and the exhale are merged with no pause in between.

Another key figure is psychiatrist Dr Stanislav Grof, one of the most important pioneers in the scientific understanding of consciousness. Using principles based on insights from modern consciousness research involving thousands of people over many years, combined with his personal experience of psychotherapy and historical spiritual practices, he created Holotropic Breathwork and co-created Transpersonal Psychology.

As you know, the technique I learned is Transformational Breath. One happy breather in one of my workshops exclaimed: 'Wow! That was like being really high on drugs. In fact, it is better than drugs.' And it's true. There's no hangover, no crash, simply a magnificent feeling of being high on the life-force energy that is our breath.

Judith Kravitz, founder and co-creator of Transformational Breath, first experienced conscious breathwork in the mid-1970s through rebirthing. She was guided to combine conscious connected breathwork with other techniques, and as Judith worked with her clients, she developed methods to make it effective, powerful and lasting.

She noticed a lot of breathwork techniques were focusing on breathing in the chest only. Judith combined techniques to open the whole respiratory system, bringing the breathing into the lower abdominals, mid and upper chest sections to create an open breath in a wave-like motion.

Over time, she combined conscious breathing, body-mapping (which involves gentle acupressure), affirmations, movement and sound, and she named her new process Transformational Breath.

This unique collection of self-healing factors helps us to correct restricted breathing patterns and let go of trapped emotions, unprocessed life experiences, blockages, negative thought tapes, belief systems and patterns that are no longer serving us. This in turn enables us to reduce stress, increase energy, heighten self-awareness, heal emotional trauma and feel more connected.

....

*Breath is the bridge which connects life to consciousness, which
unites your body to your thoughts. Whenever your mind becomes
scattered, use your breath as the means to take hold of your
mind again.*

Thich Nhat Hanh, spiritual leader and peace activist

....

The curse of modern life

Modern living is creating 'burnout' as people struggle to balance work commitments, lifestyle and family life. There is a
lot of pressure in today's society for everyone to perform, and
there seems to be just one pace of life – fast.

Sometimes we literally forget to take a breath. 'I'm so
stressed out, I can't breathe' and 'I just need some space to
breathe' are familiar refrains. This is where meditation, mindfulness and other breathing techniques come in as effective
methods of reducing stress and pain.

The pattern goes a bit like this: life happens, we are multi-
tasking, hitting deadlines, situations put us under pressure.
As a result, we are burning more energy than we need to.
We are instinctively transported into fight-or-flight mode,
preparing either to forcibly resist or run away. Stimulation,
activity and demands are all around us. We are on high-
speed-runaway-train mode and our responsibilities, commitments and worries prevent us from feeling calm and staying
in the moment.

Is it any wonder that there is an alarming rise in mental
illness and people being medicated for anxiety, depression,

burnout, stress and panic attacks? According to recent sta-
tistics from the UK Health and Safety Executive, 428,000
people reported experiencing work-related stress at a level
they believe was making them ill, accounting for 40% of
all work-related illness. Many people today feel lost, disillusioned and disconnected. Some appear to have everything
but still feel something is missing and are constantly search-
ing for it.

Internationally renowned speaker, teacher and breath
expert Max Strom sums it up thus:

> People feel more alone, even though there are more ways to
> communicate than ever; internet, social media, phones. The
> World Health Organisation has stated that by 2020, depression
> and anxiety will be the number one disability. In the United
> States, 25% of women are taking anti-depressants, anti-anxiety
> pills, or both . . . Sleep dysfunction is at an epidemic level.

Conscious breathing is a good place to start. Just as we don't
analyse how our digestive system is working or why we blink
our eyes, we don't think about breathing either. It's automatic, it just happens, doesn't it? Well, yes and no. Breathing
is different because unlike other parts of our anatomy, we can
control how we breathe and can learn to breathe consciously.
With happiness in our 21st-century society at an all-time low,
could there be a better time to try?

Self-medication

People self-medicate to get more energy or to numb and suppress their feelings. We turn to caffeine, alcohol, food, drugs, TV, porn, even shopping to alter the way we feel and take ourselves out of the uncomfortable stresses of the day-to-day.

I know from experience the short-term benefits you can experience from self-medication. I am not advocating a whiter-than-white existence, sitting on a mountain meditating all day – the majority of us don't have the time or inclination to do that, and in any case, 'everything in moderation' is a pretty good rule of thumb.

But when we are reaching mindlessly for these things to make ourselves feel good again and again, it's time to think about connecting to the breath and checking in with what part of ourselves really wants those short-term solutions before we actively pursue them.

Everyday mini thought battles

The majority of the population spends around 95% of the day thinking about things that don't matter. We have up to 50,000 thoughts a day, and that's a huge margin for random, meaningless and pointless stuff as well as more practical worries.

'What shall I have for dinner tonight?'
'Now what am I looking for again?'
'Is it too early for wine?'
'I'd really like to be on a beach right now. I'm too stressed.'

'Why can't I look as good as her?'

'How can this be happening in the world?'

'Why am I so tired?'

'I should go to yoga tonight. I know I'll feel better if I do, but I'm too tired.'

'Why do we refer to the birds and the bees when talking about sex?'

'What am I going to wear on Saturday? What if it rains? Should I plan two outfits?'

'I wonder when I'm going to get paid.'

'Okay, next week I am going to start my detox.'

'Why do we never see baby pigeons?'

'Oh, I wish I hadn't said that. I hope she didn't take it the wrong way.'

'Where does our wee go when we are on a plane?'

'How am I going to get through these exams? I'll have another cup of tea and then start studying.'

'Does my bum look big in this dress?'

'I don't want to go to the party. I won't know what to say to anyone.'

'I'm having such a great time, I don't want to leave.'

'I might post this picture on Facebook, but will anyone like it?'

'I'll just check Facebook again.'

'I'll make myself another cup of tea.'

Then there is the big stuff.

'What we are doing here?'

'Who are we?'

'What is the fundamental purpose of our lives?'

Our mind arrogantly assumes it is the master of the universe, but once we grasp that the mind is not our master and listen instead to the important messages from our hearts and bodies, we naturally become lighter and can comprehend what we truly want from life.

How we breathe depending on the situation

Every emotional state has a corresponding breath pattern. For example, in a state of joy your breathing will be relaxed, free-flowing and completely different to when you are in a heightened state of stress. In anger, we hold our breath or it speeds up, and when we feel fearful our hearts race.

Breath is the anchor to our present moment and by consciously breathing, you can influence what you are experiencing and regain control.

Breath is everywhere

The connection between spirit and life is one of those problems involving factors of such complexity . . . For how can we bring into the orbit of our thought those limitless complexities of life which we call 'Spirit' or 'Life' unless we clothe them in verbal concepts, themselves mere counters of the intellect? . . . 'Spirit' and 'Life' are familiar enough words to us, very old acquaintances in fact, pawns that for thousands of years have been pushed back and forth on the thinker's chessboard. The problem must have begun in the grey dawn of time, when someone made the bewildering discovery that the living breath which left the body of the dying man in the last death-rattle meant more than just air in motion.

C. G. Jung, psychotherapist and psychiatrist

The relationship between breath and emotion is often used in phrases such as 'She breathed a sigh of relief', 'The landscape was breathtaking', 'The first time I saw him, he took my breath away', and 'Let's take a breather'. The word 'conspire' comes from two Latin words literally meaning breathe together. The English word 'spirit' comes from the Latin *spiritus*, which is inextricably linked with our spirit, soul, courage and vigour.

Kim, 37, is an opera singer. This is her story.

I once read that 'the plan will reveal itself to you when you are ready to see it'. I didn't believe in plans. But I did believe society's message that I was part of the generation that could 'have it all'.

I put off having children until my mid-30s and focused instead on being a hardworking 21st-century woman. I had a successful career as an opera singer, a great husband, wonderful friends, a beautiful home, and travelled often.

When the time came to start a family, I worked very hard at it. However, after four years, I found that I was working hard at 'failing' to get pregnant, and suddenly, I was the woman who couldn't 'have it all' after all.

I had some tests and my doctor told me that I had the reproductive system of a 20-year-old, but I didn't jump for joy, because unexplained infertility as a childless 37-year-old woman is not much of a consolation prize. Instead, I felt angry that I had this perfectly healthy body that couldn't perform the fundamental function of reproduction.

I tried everything: ashtanga yoga, meditation, ayurveda, a strict diet, and attended endless self-development talks along the way, but nothing worked. The IVF waiting list was over a year long, and the thought of not being able to have children was devastating.

I could feel myself slipping into a dark abyss with no way out. Society went from telling me I could 'have it all' to telling me I had to 'hurry up' because I was rapidly losing time. Bar moving to an ashram in India, I didn't know what else to try – but you can't have sex in an ashram, so even that was out!

My husband read an article about Transformational Breath and I thought: 'Let's try it.' I booked us in for a group session. The specialised rhythmic breathing technique was challenging, unlike anything I'd experienced in yoga or singing, but once we got into the rhythm, it immediately brought up many emotions, as well as tears.

Leaving the group session, my husband and I simply looked at each other in shock and walked home in silence. That night, we both had fitful sleep peppered with intense dreams about our past. We were intrigued and decided to arrange a few one-on-one sessions with Rebecca the following month.

The sessions weren't easy. The breath brought up emotional and physical sensations that were difficult to fathom. However, the most difficult thing about the session was setting an honest intention. I found myself trying to impress Rebecca, and therein lay my problem. I am a very private person and that manifested itself in telling her what I thought she'd like to hear rather than what I really felt.

The combination of breath and intention was like watching my truth hurtle full speed at me through a gaping portal. Each session was like peeling away a layer of an onion. I released fresh, stinging tears of anger, regret and guilt for becoming a person I no longer recognised. I had become addicted to fear, stress and self-loathing following a challenging childhood, and had spent my entire life using an all-or-nothing approach to struggle to propel me to succeed. Having children was just another struggle to overcome in my mind.

Transformational Breath brought me the clarity to realise that this struggle was not useful. With every session, I felt a gradual lifting of stress. I started getting more rest, exercising less frenetically, eating well and working less hard.

This shift became obvious to me when I went on a demanding one-woman opera tour. Usually, I would have squeezed the life out of the music and myself with meticulous preparation and practice, leaving not much leeway for further discoveries. This time, however, I did just enough work to create a real space of learning and development. The strategy paid off, the tour was a tremendous success, and I felt an overwhelming sense of self-love and acceptance. Despite the intense nature of the project, I was not left completely spent emotionally and physically at the end of it.

Something even more surprising happened after the tour. I discovered I was pregnant.

Clearing this blockage increased my creativity, too. I've become more open to music projects outside opera, and have been writing and recording an album with a band. I've also learned to drive and have completed an MA.

It's difficult to believe that these positive shifts could be attributed to using a specific breathing technique, but the connection is undeniable. When things don't go my way in future, I will turn to Transformational Breath to support me.

Early breathing patterns

Most of us are not using our whole respiratory system to breathe. In fact, many of us use just 33%, a mere third of our total capacity. The next time you look at a newborn baby as they sleep, take note of the way their whole body is breathing and how their breathing is connected. Their back, tummy and chest move together with no blockages.

Toddlers usually breathe into their chests and their bellies. The breath moves consistently, like an ocean wave ebbing and flowing.

Each human being is unique, with a unique breathing pattern illustrating our story, where we are in the world, and how we perceive ourselves. Everyone's breathing has a story that encompasses birth trauma, early childhood experiences, parental authority, school peers, and angst from our teenage years and early adulthood.

Our 20s should be the best period of our lives, as we experience independence, spread our wings, and embark on a rewarding path, but we often don't feel we know who we are or what our purpose is in life. It makes sense that when we clear these areas in the subconscious mind we create room for peace in our lives and receive the insights that we ask for.

So what kind of breather are you?

Some of us are chest breathers while others are belly breathers. Then there are those who breathe more in the midsection. By opening and clearing the restricted breathing pattern, we can breathe more freely and easily.

Our breath represents how we flow in life. As we open and expand our breath, we have more energy and support for the body's natural healing abilities. Our primary breathing muscles are the diaphragm, intercostals, scalenes and abdominals, yet some of us are working really hard with the upper chest muscles, which creates tension here. There can be tightness in the diaphragm, which is attached to the deep-seated core muscle, the psoas (from the Greek word meaning 'loin region'), and if this becomes tight, the hips also become constricted.

Conduct a little experiment by looking at the breathing patterns of people around you. Can you notice if they are breathing more into their belly or their chest? Are they inhaling deeply and fully into their belly? Is their exhale easy to release? Does their breath seem shallow? Do they blow or push the exhale out? And which is longer, the inhale or exhale?

If we consider the way we breathe a metaphor for how we live our lives, it becomes obvious that as we restrict our flow of breath, we impede our natural flow. By focusing our intention on redirecting the breath, we begin to experience a relationship with our life force, our creative power. Once we revive this creative flow, we begin to nurture our bodies and minds, and the fear and pain we've internalised as a result of toxins or destructive thought patterns is transformed into love and joy.

⊨ EXERCISE ⊨

ARE YOU A BELLY BREATHER OR A CHEST BREATHER?

You can do this sitting up straight or lying down.

If you're sitting up, keep your spine straight.

Relax your shoulders, but try not to hunch them.

Close your eyes.

Take a deep inhale through the nose and let go of the exhale through the nose.

Repeat this two or three times, breathing in and breathing out.

Now place one hand on your belly and the other hand on your chest.

Breathe in through the nose and out through the nose.

Notice where you can feel the breath more.

Can you feel it more in your chest or can you feel it more in your belly?

⊨⊨

A guide to breath patterns

Shallow breather

We become shallow breathers during periods of stress, when
we are depressed, when we've not had much sleep, have had
a bad day at work or the kids are playing up.

Chest breather

If you breathe in the upper chest, you could be an overthink-
er who spends a lot of time in your head. If the heart area is
closed, you may be protecting yourself in relationships or in
life from being hurt. Often, this leads to holding back from
true passion and relates to our connection to our heart and
to the ability to do what we love.

Belly breather

Those who are not breathing in their bellies often don't
feel grounded and can be a bit spaced out. This category of
breathers often has strong-willed parents and tends to consist
of people-pleasers who put others before themselves and
experience low self-esteem. Belly breathing is our connection
to personal will and power. Belly breathers tend to be more
grounded and present. When breathing in our belly, we are
more connected to our body.

Frozen breath

Donna Farhi's *The Breathing Book* describes frozen breathing as a time when 'the entire outer layer of the body contracts and suppresses the rising movement of the breath'. When you breathe freely, the inner contents and outer contents move with one another. In frozen breathing, the outer container remains rigid.

> This pattern is common in people who are very goal-oriented. 'Getting there' always supersedes 'being here'. Such a person appears smaller than they really are, especially in the way they draw their shoulders in toward each other. These people will hold their breaths in any number of situations and often rationalize their tensions by saying 'As soon as this is over, *then* I'll relax!' Such a person is often so concerned with getting things right and achieving his goals, that he is willing to literally stop breathing to get there. The root of this pattern is fear – fear of not being good enough, fear of not getting there, and fear of not becoming someone.
>
> Frozen breathing can also be a consequence of having lived in great fear for an extended period of time . . . Children who have been physically or sexually abused, veterans suffering post-traumatic stress syndrome, and others who have lived through devastating experiences may freeze their body and breath as a way of coping with overwhelming feelings . . . The person must be allowed to open at his own pace so that the feelings that will inevitably arise can be integrated rather than overwhelming him as they did in the past.

Once we can clear these areas for a full, open breath, we feel lighter, clearer and more energised. Ultimately, we want a full, open breath and, as with all things, with practice this can be achieved. The more we practise, the more we let go of the restricted breathing patterns and old holding habits.

Aimee, 41, is a conscious breathworker and yoga teacher. This is her story.

'You are not breathing fully,' stated the Balinese yoga teacher, looking at my lower belly with a bemused expression on his face.

'How could this be?' I thought. I had spent the past 4 years fully immersed in back-to-back yoga teacher training. I had spent hours practising pranayama to the dawn chorus, evenings at conscious breath workshops, hours attempting to master routine asana, all with the promise of expanding my breath. At the weekends I regularly attended Kundalini yoga classes, where it was all about the breath.

After all this practice, how could I possibly not be breathing fully? He looked almost sorry for me as he deadpanned: 'Your belly is not rising properly. It's weak.' I loved the Balinese for their honesty but I couldn't understand what he meant.

After 3 months in my dream job, teaching yoga in an idyllic mountainside yoga studio, I had to leave Bali, but the teacher's words travelled home with me. Back in London, I landed a job within a week, and a poster at my new yoga studio caught my eye. 'Transformational Breath can help access a full respiratory system.' I booked a session.

In my first session, under the professional gaze of a fully

trained breathing expert, I gained a full understanding of how I was breathing. Throughout my yoga teacher training, and in every class I'd been to before or since, from the Balinese mountains of Tegallalang to London's renowned Triyoga, not once had we turned our focus to our individual breathing patterns. I learned that we all breathe in a completely unique way. This was a revelation.

I learned that a yoga pose will feel very different to someone with a slightly different breath-holding pattern to me. I was an upper-chest breather. My intercostal muscles were tight, my shoulder muscles were overused, and my diaphragm was not moving to its full potential. In one private session, I was able to access how it felt to have a full diaphragmatic breath, and suddenly my body fell into this deep hypnotic state of relaxation. I remember saying at the end of the session when asked to open my eyes, 'No, please let me stay in this state for ever.' My whole body was buzzing and I could sense exactly what I was: trillions of cells vibrating, and while my attention was on this new intense sensation, my mind became calm and still.

I was accessing states I had never known were possible, fascinated and intrigued by my newfound knowledge that everyone's breath pattern is as unique as their thumbprint. I signed up to train as a facilitator the very next day. The training was thorough, especially the breathing analysis, and before long, while teaching my normal yoga class, I was noticing everyone's breathing patterns. People in my yoga class were holding beautiful poses but not one person was breathing properly. I suddenly realised through my own experience that you have to be taught how to really breathe deeply. The muscles in the respiratory system need to be activated to fully let go of any tension. Yoga will help this to some extent, but I was passionate about teaching everyone to breathe fully first. Yoga poses could come later.

Transformational Breath arrived at the perfect time in my life. Much more than a simple relaxation technique, it has helped me to overcome anxiety, to navigate calmly through relationship break-ups and make-ups, and it was my go-to practice during pregnancy. It was my crutch while suffering mild postnatal depression, and it gives me energy, insight and inspiration. It has changed my life. My belief is that everyone should learn to correct unhealthy breathing patterns before learning any other breathing exercises. The benefits of other breathing exercises go much deeper and last much longer if you understand why you breathe the way you do.

Going back to our roots

Once we have begun to open the breath, we can start to understand the reasons why we shut down our breathing in the first place. The body remembers everything, holding on to repressed and suppressed emotions on a cellular level. Negative beliefs, old tapes, past memories, trapped or blocked energy, they are all lingering inside, stuck in the subconscious in our bid to shut down and control our breathing.

Our fight-or-flight system is very useful if we are trying to flee from a situation. This is supposed to be a transient state, yet some of us remain in it constantly when our systems get confused and go into overdrive. Think of it this way: our knee-jerk reaction when we experience traumatic or stressful events in life is to hold on to our breath. Our animal instinct kicks in but sometimes we remain stuck in survival mode.

In ancient times, when humans were threatened by a predator like a sabre-toothed tiger, the adrenaline and cortisol levels would rise, fuel would be released in our bodies, and we would either kill or we'd be eaten.

In Peter A. Levine's book *In an Unspoken Voice* he explains that when a herd of gazelles in the wild is being chased, each animal is acutely attuned to the danger and is prepared to act decisively to meet it: 'The snap of a twig, the rustling of some bushes, a fleeting shadow or a few molecules of a particular scent alert one member of the herd.' The gazelle pauses, 'giving it an opportunity to organize an optimal escape route. In addition, the other animals of the herd instantly attune to its postural shift by arresting their activity as well. They all scan *together* (many more ears, noses and eyes), better to localize and identify the source of threat. There is a similar response to potential threat from an army squad on patrol in enemy territory.' They flee, and once they know they are safe, their bodies begin to shake and they release any trauma of that event immediately. Then they return to grazing in as calm a state as they were before. It is a natural, innate process that all mammals possess which keeps their nervous systems in a relaxed state.

Humans are the only mammals who have a cognitive brain, the part that rationalises, justifies and can override our instinctual responses. This is where humans get stuck. We overthink things rather than follow our instincts and listen to our body.

While animals go into fight-or-flight mode only when their lives are in danger, us humans will invoke it in far less threatening scenarios. We may receive an unpleasant email, for example, be given an unrealistic deadline at work, or get irate about traffic issues, and this can be all it takes for the stress chemicals in our body to react and rise.

Suddenly, we are in a state of heightened anxiety. If we haven't had a call from someone we were expecting to hear from, every time the phone rings we will feel our heart begin to race. If we hear that someone has been saying unpleasant things about us or if someone is being rude about someone we love, we react in our body to these actions and the rhythm of our breath changes.

The healing process

A traumatic event can be a wake-up call, as with every painful experience there is a chance to gain strength and make a choice. What is important is the individual's capacity to respond to the event and how we hold that trauma in the body. Some people heal more readily and easily than others. It's as though our body is holding a entire filing cabinet of memories, and the data inside builds up a defence that informs how we behave in our daily lives.

We need to allow the body to let go of its defences in order to be authentic with our true selves and live life fully. In an ideal world, we would put these experiences or unwanted thoughts into a shredding machine. Instead, we are being ruled by internal fear patterns that inhibit our ability to lead a full and vital life.

Once we have begun to clear patterns in the subconscious, we can begin to open up to our higher consciousness.

Some people find spirituality uncomfortable or off-putting. Some of us pray to a god, while others feel more connected to nature, love or higher energies. Each of us is unique, with different belief systems and religions, and the experience we have with breathwork will be unique too.

Some people have profound spiritual experiences when practising breathwork, while others see colours and light. Some feel very relaxed and calm while others find it hard to come out of the mind. And some feel a closer connection to Source.

What is Source, you may ask. Like I say, we all have a different experience of an inner guide, god or connection to our spirit. You can call it whatever you want. Don't worry if this doesn't resonate with you. I also spent a lot of time questioning the whole idea when people would tell me they had spoken to their angels or their guides or had been held in a white light. I'd close my eyes thinking: 'Where are these angels then? I can't see anything!'

With time, Source came to me in a different way, but only because I eventually gave myself permission to let go of my cynical overthinking mind and surrender. This is when the magic happens.

But for now, just remember this: there is no right or wrong as to what happens. By letting go of the outside and expanding our awareness inside, we can feel peace in a place that is always home. We feel more comfortable in our skin and connect with the essence of who we really are. Who would not want that for themselves?

*One Transformational Breath session is equivalent to about two
years of psychotherapy.*

Dr Henry Smith-Rohrberg

With the breath, we can access part of the subconscious in a
way that talking therapy often cannot achieve, as our mind
cannot always express what the body is holding on to.

The way I see it, we have this wonderful medicine right
under our nose – our breath – and even better, it's free and
has no side effects! Read on for some simple breathing exercises using connected conscious breath, and other methods
and tools that you can use on your own and incorporate into
your daily life.

Nicky, 57, is a breathworker and artist. This is her story.

I came to Transformational Breath initially for health reasons. I had
endometrial cancer and believed that the breath exercises would
support me in my journey back to good health.

From the start the breathing sessions gave me more energy and
happiness, but also seemed to elicit physical sensations at old sites
of childhood illnesses or injuries such as ear infections and twisted
ankles. I smelled the antibiotics in my breath from my recent
operation, and felt a sense of chill from the anaesthetic. I was
fascinated.

As I continued to breathe, I started having visions, understandings and affirmations of personal truths. I would see or hear single images or words, other times phrases, or even entire stories played out like movies, often in symbolic format requiring gentle interpretation. They seemed more balanced, wise and compassionate than any thoughts I might have had about myself, as though they were gifted or divinely sent. The degree of wisdom and grace shown me was profoundly moving, humbling, and expanded my sense of connection with a universal soul, with God, and, in time, with all that I am.

How could this happen from just 45 minutes of focused breathing? That the access to this level of connection, expansion and healing should be available to us all via our breath, a function of our bodies that most of us take for granted, seemed too perfect and simple – like many great truths seem to be! The workshops and trainings became my path and I am now an unexpected but grateful facilitator!

Deep diaphragmatic breathing

When working with clients, I observe where their breath is and put them into a position to help them guide it either into the belly or the chest to create an open, connected breath.

The first step towards achieving a healthy breath is diaphragmatic breathing. Although deep diaphragmatic breathing is easy, you will need to let go of old patterns first for it to become automatic.

A lot of people breathe into their chest muscles rather

than fully using their diaphragm, external intercostals and the scalene muscles while relaxing the lower abdominals, which is how a quiet breath should be. Some people hold on to a lot of tension in the diaphragm, and by becoming aware of this you can release the tension held there through the breath. Chest breathing is a part of fight-or-flight when we are under extreme stress or in danger. The breath can feel rapid, irregular, jerky or shallow if we are breathing in the chest. By breathing deeply into our diaphragm, we activate the parasympathetic nervous system, leading us into a calm state.

Feeling your diaphragm

Your diaphragm is a dome-shaped sheet of muscle and tendon that serves as the main muscle of respiration and plays a vital role in the breathing process. As we breathe in, we should feel the belly expand slightly as the dome contracts and compresses the abdominal space.

As we breathe out, both the chest and belly fall. Take a moment to visualise where the diaphragm is in your body. The organs above the diaphragm need to be connected and in communication with the organs below the diaphragm, so there are openings for blood vessels and nerves.

In yoga teacher and breathing expert Donna Farhi's ground-breaking tome *The Breathing Book*, she explains how the Native Americans saw the diaphragm as the horizon between heaven and Earth. This is a fitting analogy, for above it are our inspiration and ideas and below is our grounded centre: our heart, lungs and brain reside above the diaphragm and our other organs are below.

Donna explains it thus:

When the diaphragm is moving in the luxurious expansion that marks full breathing, all the organs are massaged, rolled, churned and bathed in new blood, fluid and oxygen, getting squeezed and released like sponges. Breathing stimulates the body to work better, which is why it has such a profound effect on our sense of wellbeing.

⊨ EXERCISE ⊨

DIAPHRAGMATIC BREATHING

Lie on the floor in Shavasana or Corpse Pose, on your back with legs comfortably spread and the arms relaxed alongside the body. Feel and connect with the ground beneath your body, placing both hands on your lower abdominals just below your rib cage.

Start by focusing on the inhale and exhale and notice the rise of the inhale and the fall of the exhale. Breathing in through your nose, your belly rises, and breathing out through your nose, the belly comes down. Allow there to be a pause between each breath.

Can you feel the breath in your belly? If not, try bending your knees, keeping your feet on the ground. This will help the breath to come down into the lower abdominals.

Can you feel the rise and fall of your belly as you breathe? Imagine as you inhale that there is a balloon inside or a ball of light expanding with each breath. This is a deep diaphragmatic breath.

If you are having difficulties feeling the breath in your belly then you can try this: find a heavy book or a large bag of rice. Place this on your belly and put your hands on top.

Now as you inhale, gently push the weighty object into your hands and keep it there as you breathe in and out. You can ask a friend or family member to observe you while you are doing this.

If you are not finding it easy to get the breath into your belly or the observer is not seeing the rise or fall of your belly, try Crocodile Pose.

Crocodile Pose

Lie on your stomach and place your legs a comfortable distance apart, pointing the toes outwards.

Fold your arms in front of you and place your forehead on your arms so that your chest is not touching the floor.

As you inhale, feel your abdominal muscles pressing against the floor and imagine that there is a balloon in your belly or a ball of light expanding with each breath.

As you exhale, feel the abdominals relaxing. This will help to bring the breath into the belly. Take a few breaths in this position.

The red pill or the blue pill?

Josh, 32, was working in the City as a trader and his pace of life was very fast. He was extremely good at his job and loved the 'work hard, play hard' lifestyle, but his body began sending red flags and soon he reached burnout.

By the time he came to see me, he was on medication for depression and anxiety, and although he was still working in the City, his company had moved him to a different department on the advice of their in-house psychiatrist.

Josh's new job involved sitting at a desk crunching numbers and analysing data, and he found it hard to stay focused and engaged after the adrenaline rush of working on the trading floor.

His psychiatrist recommended a pill that was new to the market and had been developed for people like Josh. He would be a guinea pig, and the hope was that the new medication would help to rewire his brain to focus and adapt to his new work pace. (While Western medicine can and does save lives, it's worrying to hear of new medication being prescribed with no warning about potential long-term side effects.)

The first thing I noticed was that Josh's breath showed a control pattern and fear pattern being held in his diaphragm. He wasn't grounded or present and he found it extremely hard to get out of his mind and dismiss the constant litany of thoughts going through his head. It was a challenge to get his breath down into his tummy because his diaphragm was too tense.

We conducted the first couple of sessions with him lying

in Crocodile Pose so that he could guide the breath down. I was able to help him release some of the tension being held in his back and diaphragm, and soon he was able to relax more into the breath.

After a couple of sessions, he could lie on his back and breathe into his belly in a more natural, relaxed way. He began to think about the recent transitions in his life and started to reassess what was important to him. Materially, he was successful and had no money worries, and breathwork helped him to look closely and fearlessly at his life, let go of negative patterns, and realise that by changing the world inside him, he could change the world around him too.

⊨ EXERCISE ⊨

BREATH IS OUR ANCHOR

A simple exercise to help you focus and feel more present.

If you are having difficulty staying present, begin by allowing your mind to wander to the breath.

When we have lots of thoughts buzzing around, it's very hard to stay focused and often we don't know where to begin. Begin with the breath.

As you breathe in and breathe out, wander around the body with your breath. Notice where the breath follows and stay with the flow of air coming in and out of your body.

Direct your focus inwards and continue to allow the mind to wander around the body with your breath.

Ask yourself: 'What is going on inside me right now? What do I need to achieve? Not tomorrow, not later on, in this moment which is NOW.'

Breathe into this thought and stay focused on the breath, bringing you back into the now. Breath anchors us in the now.

———

John, 32, is a teacher and a therapist. This is his story.

'You're going to see Rebecca?' Oh gosh, you will love her. It's amazing, you'll cry!'

My friend who'd recommended Transformational Breath with Rebecca was right. My time with her has been amazing and I have cried. My arrival onto Rebecca's mat was part of a much longer journey through breakdown, depression, relapse and, finally, recovery.

Five years ago, I was stumbling through life, trying my best on the outside and crumbling on the inside. My problem was I couldn't see or feel inwardly; my pain, emptiness, fear and terror were all shut down inside me.

I held in my feelings, hiding a private world of shameful secrets, and compensated for this by striving to be perfect at work. I was split between an impeccable persona during the working week and losing myself in a hedonistic spiral of alcohol, parties, drugs and sex at the weekend.

Early stressful life events and trauma, anger in the home and bullying at school happened to me at a time when I was too young to know how to cope. I was unaware that I am the child of two wounded parents, who were also the children of wounded parents, and that there was little in the way of secure coping strategies to pass on. I wasn't conscious of family secrets and sexual abuse, which were generational wounds I carried.

In June 2011, my mind and body finally cracked, and at the start of a dance performance in London, I walked out of the theatre in the midst of a psychotic episode. Two days later I was admitted to a psychiatric ward and detained under the Mental Health Act.

I was scared and alone, but in the clinic I began to take part in music, art and group therapy. I met my first CBT and mindfulness-based psychologist, who helped me get out of hospital, out of my flat, back on public transport and back to work – no mean feat considering that these day-to-day things now terrified me and had to be relearned one by one.

It took a few years before I started to enjoy life again, have hopes and dreams and allow myself to fantasise about a better future. My inner light came back on, and I decided I wanted to bring more meaning into my professional life and work closer with humanity. I loved teaching, but decided to become a therapist and started training.

On my friend's recommendation, I booked a Transformational Breath session with Rebecca. I immediately felt relaxed. After discussing a little of my history, she looked at my breathing and read my experience. She commented on my shallow upper breathing and asked: 'Do you struggle with perfectionism?' I felt moved to tears.

Rebecca made affirmations, telling me that it's okay to love myself, and gently encouraged me. At the end of the first session, I felt a deep, serene peace, which became a theme of my sessions.

My most powerful experience came in my fifth breathing session. I had experienced a brief relapse of psychotic symptoms, and when I finally returned for the session, I felt I had completed a huge inner journey. My last relapse was the first occasion during which, despite acute symptoms, I was able to stay at home and receive care out of hospital to recover with the support of family and friends.

Many years ago, in Chile, I visited a healer who said that one of the secrets to health was finding 'tu ancla', your anchor. She showed me hers, which consisted of a deep, slow breath in and out while holding her hands together across her belly. I forgot about that experience, and without finding my anchor I was susceptible to being blown around, emotionally and mentally, every now and again. Rebecca's passionate encouragement to rediscover my anchor brought back that memory. Breathing into my anchor has become an important feature of my daily practice.

Breathwork has helped me feel: feel into my breath, feel into my body, into my pain and into my potential. I can honestly say I am learning to love myself.

Breath Is Medicine

NOTICE YOUR BREATH

Close your eyes, sitting up straight and lengthening the spine.

Feel your hips and your sitting bones on the seat. Feel your feet on the ground beneath you.

Scan over your body and notice how your body and your breath feels today.

Does it feel shallow or is it flowing? Is it quick or does it feel laboured? Can you feel any tightness in your body? Can you feel any restrictions in your breath? Can you feel the breath in your tummy or in your chest area?

Now begin to breathe in and breathe out. Allow the breath to enter softly through the nose and out of the mouth.

As you inhale, direct the breath into your tummy, visualising filling the space with air. As you inhale, the belly expands and as you exhale, the belly goes in. Take a few deep breaths here, inhale and exhale with a little pause in between.

Continue to focus your awareness on the belly. Place one hand there and breathe into your hand, pushing it gently away with your inhale, expanding your breath and then guiding it inwards with your exhale. Allow the mind to wander to your breath.

Feel the rib cage expand and contract as you breathe. Practise this for one or two minutes.

Notice how your breath feels and notice how your body feels.

Come back to your normal breathing pattern, breathing through your nose. Note how your body feels and how your breath feels.

Open your eyes. Take a deep breath in through the nose and let it go with a big sigh out of the mouth.

Conscious breathing

As you read this book, you will gradually become more aware of your breath in everyday life and therefore become more present. You may notice that you have just got through a whole sentence or written an email and not taken a breath.

You may be walking along a country lane or standing in a queue waiting for a coffee and you will begin to notice your breath. If you are running, swimming, dancing or horse-riding, take note that by becoming aware of your breath and breathing deeply and consciously into the belly, this method of breathing with awareness will become more natural and will help you to move more freely and feel more relaxed.

⊨ EXERCISE ⊨

DEEP BELLY-BREATHING GROUNDING EXERCISE

This simple exercise is very similar to the previous one and takes a couple of minutes. By helping you to connect to the breath in your body and encouraging the breath into your belly, this exercise is easy to do any time you feel a little anxious or you need to become calm and focused. Try it and notice the difference after.

Close your eyes, sitting up straight and lengthening the spine. Feel your hips and your sitting bones on the seat. Feel your feet on the ground beneath you. Imagine that your feet are rooted to the ground.

Scan over your body and notice how your body feels and how your breath feels. Is it shallow or flowing? Is it quick or does it feel laboured? Can you feel any tightness in your body or any restrictions in your breath? Can you feel the breath in your tummy or in your chest area?

Now begin to breathe in and breathe out. Allow the breath to enter softly through the nose and out of the mouth.

As you inhale, direct the breath into your tummy, filling the space with air. As you inhale, the belly expands and as you exhale, the belly goes in. Take a few deep breaths, inhale and exhale with a little pause in between. Keep your focus on the inhale and the exhale and allow your mind to wander to the breath in your belly.

Continue to bring your awareness to the belly and place one hand there and breathe into your hand, pushing it gently away with your inhale, expanding your belly with your breath and then guiding it inwards with your exhale. Let go of your thoughts and as thoughts come in, gently push them aside.

Use affirmations such as 'I feel calm and focused', 'I am freeing my mind and letting go of any negative thoughts.'

Feel the rib cage expand and contract as you breathe. Practise this for one or two minutes. Notice how your breath feels and how your body feels.

Now come back to your normal breathing pattern, breathing through your nose. Notice how your body feels and your breath feels. Open your eyes, take a deep breath in through the nose and let it go with a big sigh out of the mouth.

Setting a practice

Conscious breathing or conscious connected breathing refers to breathing with an intention or purpose. When using conscious breath exercises it is beneficial to set intentions on what we would like to achieve, such as feeling relaxed or having more clarity or focus.

I suggest you make the intention a positive one rather than including negative words such as 'letting go of fear'. If that is what you would like to achieve, try not thinking these negative words during the session, and instead imagine letting go of them and focus on how that would give you more confidence or courage.

By taking our awareness to our breath, letting go of our thoughts and focusing only on the rhythm of the inhale and the exhale, we are brought back into the moment. This can be difficult to master at first, but with regular practice it becomes easier and more achievable. I often get my best ideas straight after a breathing session, as I have switched off my overthinking mind, creating space for creativity to flow.

I recommend practising breathing exercises every day. Sometimes I will practise for only five minutes, using the exercises I've included in this book, and other times I'll practise for longer. I always set an intention for the day, particularly if I'm asking for answers when my mind feels unclear. It's not unusual to feel unfocused or lose our way at times. We can feel differently from one minute to the next, day to day. Setting intentions and practising breathing exercises helps to centre us and bring us back to the present.

When setting intentions, I ask myself:

'What do I want to let go of?'

'What would be meaningful for me today?'

'What action do I need to take in order to be the best version of myself and feel comfortable in myself?'

'How do I want to feel today?'

'What energy do I want to feel, no matter what happens in my day?'

If something is unresolved and you can't see an answer, the breath helps you to become the observer, taking yourself out of the story and offering a different perspective.

Take a deep breath and ask what your heart wants and

go with the first word or phrase that comes up. Try not to engage too much with the mind, and make your intention doable and realistic. It's not realistic to expect enlightenment to be delivered in one five-minute session, so please don't feel disappointed if this doesn't happen.

Often messages or insights can come after the sessions, somewhere totally unexpected. Perhaps you'll be out doing some shopping or on a run when a very clear message comes through. What we are doing is making space for them to appear, once the unnecessary clutter is cleared from our busy minds. There is no right or wrong. And if you can't think of an intention, that's okay too. Just set an intention to simply stay present with each breath.

Find a time in the day that works for you. Some people find it easier to do first thing in the morning, while others prefer last thing at night. Play around and see when works best. If you live in a busy household, the morning option may not be realistic unless you get up before everyone else. A great place to practise breathing exercises is in the bath. Close the door and light some candles to create the right ambience. Make sure you're not going to be interrupted. And *please*, turn off your phone.

Make time for five minutes of practice a day and you will notice a difference. If possible, create a breathing space for yourself in your home. If this is not possible due to space, don't worry, you can breathe on your bed or in your living room. There will be times when that five minutes feels like it's flown by and other times when it feels like an hour. Try not to be disheartened if you feel distracted.

I often use music but it's not necessary, and some people

prefer silence. If you are using music, choose a piece that will take you on an inward journey. If I want to feel energised or shift energy that feels heavy, I'll choose African drumming music, and if I want to clear my head and feel more connected, I'll opt for a more ambient style. Try to avoid music with lyrics as this can draw your attention – or try music with lyrics in a foreign language. I have recommended music to breathe to at the end of the book if you are struggling to find some yourself.

How practice can help you

When we are feeling stuck or under pressure to make an important decision quickly, it's perfectly natural to react from a place of fear or to become easily overwhelmed. Setting intentions and breathing consciously for a few minutes each day can help us to break those habits of the mind that hold us back.

Sarah is 36 and self-employed.

Recently, I received an email that really upset me and immediately I wanted to reply with a harsh response. I had been asked to choose between two people I love very much and it made me feel very angry. I decided to take myself off for a 20-minute breathing session before responding.

I stayed with the emotion that I was feeling in my body and breathed through it, not analysing the situation but just staying present with my breath and the feeling of that emotion. By the end of the session, I felt very calm and had a totally different perspective on the issue. I stepped away from the drama of the situation and then calmly replied asking not to be forced into making a choice – which was a totally different response to the one I would have made had I not taken myself off for a breathing session.

The mind is like water. Sometimes it's still and calm like a beautiful lake. When we throw in a pebble (a thought), this creates little ripples. At other times, it can be a murky, stormy, turbulent sea. When it settles, it becomes clear again.

> *Be like water making its way through cracks. Do not be assertive, but adjust to the object, and you shall find a way around or through it . . . Empty your mind, be formless. Shapeless, like water. Be water, my friend.*
>
> Bruce Lee

When embarking on a daily breathing practice and setting an intention, ask yourself what it is you would like more of in your life: what does your heart yearn for? And don't beat yourself up if you don't manage to practise every day. When people set themselves new things to do, it can sometimes feel like another chore. We have all these good intentions to meditate, do yoga, create mood boards, go to the gym, start a detox and so on, and we are bound to fall off the wagon every now and then. When I first started I would feel guilty if I missed a couple of days, but it's important not to go into self-critical mode. Each day is a new day, and even if it takes you a while to master a practice and genuinely fall in love with it, so be it.

⊨ EXERCISE ⊨

DEEP-RELEASE BREATH EXERCISE

Inhale through the nose and then exhale through the mouth.

Allow every breath in to be calm and slow. At the top of the inhale, release the air through the open mouth, relax and pause. Patiently and consciously wait until the body breathes again.

Remember to keep the breath in the belly. As you inhale, the belly and the rib cage expand, and as you exhale, the belly contracts.

The key here is in the pause between breaths and in remaining conscious, focused and purposeful while waiting until the body chooses to inhale. If the mind wanders, bring it back to the breath.

During each pause, allow your body to deeply relax and let go. Let the time between each breath be a time to let the whole body release.

Identify where any tension is in the body, breathe into this part of the body, and consciously feel the tension releasing and letting go.

Use two fingers to find your breast bone, which is the sternum, and then trace down the sternum (the bone in the centre of your chest) until you reach the central point of the rib cage. Guide your finger a couple of centimetres down from the sternum. Place your two fingers on that point and apply gentle pressure on the exhale and then release on the inhale. Make sure your fingers are not on the bone but just below. This is your solar plexus area.

Repeat affirmations in your head as you breathe in and out: 'I let go. I trust and I let go.'

Practise this for a minute or two.

Now let your head fall to the right and hang there and feel the release in the left side of your neck and shoulder. Apply gentle pressure with two fingers along the trapezius muscle on the top of your shoulder. Use gentle pressure on the exhale and release on the inhale.

Affirm that 'I let go of any tension I am holding on to here.' We tend to hold on to responsibility in our shoulders, and if we are sitting at a desk for a long time, we can feel a build-up of tension. Give yourself permission with each exhale to let go of any tension that you may be holding.

Practise this for a minute or two and then repeat on the other side. The shoulders should feel freer and lighter as the tension in your neck is released.

Now bring your head back to the centre and continue inhaling through the nose and letting go of the exhale through the mouth.

Take a deep breath in through the nose and let the exhale go with a big sigh out of your mouth. Do this three more times and notice how your body feels.

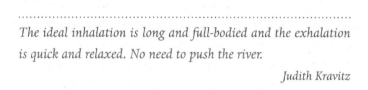

Holding patterns

The ideal inhalation is long and full-bodied and the exhalation is quick and relaxed. No need to push the river.

Judith Kravitz

By asking our body to relax each time we exhale, we unwind stored tension. Often people hold on to the inhalation or force or push the exhale out, which can signify a fear of letting go.

Those of us who are not breathing in our chests may be protecting our emotions. It doesn't necessarily mean we are emotionally cut off, but there may be something we are protecting in our heart area stemming perhaps from fear of not being loved or not wanting to be hurt, or feelings of grief or loss.

When people are not breathing in their bellies, they can feel unearthed. In terms of energy, the abdomen is the seat of our power and subconscious. Not breathing in this area can lead to digestive or lower back issues. Abdominal breathers tend to be more grounded, in tune with their bodies and exert more power to get the job done, whereas shallow breathers can feel spaced out or find it difficult to focus.

If we are very emotional but not very grounded, we can have lots of ideas spinning around. We get excited about one idea and then wander to another idea but find it hard to get these ideas off the ground. By understanding this, the breath can help us to find that balance.

Another example is the people-pleaser pattern, which usually stems from early childhood and the desire to please our parents or peers (naturally, the pattern shows in our breath). Later on in life, continuing to put others before ourselves can be draining and frustrating. We may feel resentful or bitter that we are being taken advantage of, yet we find ourselves gravitating back to these negative patterns.

Think of the breath as a musical instrumental, a guitar or a flute perhaps, which needs to be kept in tune with our body to keep us in the flow of life. When it flows, our life flows too.

Our breath helps us gauge how comfortable (or uncomfortable) we are at any given moment. When we are afraid, we tighten our bodies and breathe faster; when relaxed, we soften and breathe slowly.

As you will read, from an early age, Lexi had to become acutely connected to all her senses and intuition. Often this works to her advantage, but at other times it has left her feeling fearful. Through breathwork she was able to let go, and strip away the trauma and fear being held in her body. If people ever doubt the power of breathwork, they should watch a session with Lexi and her guide dog, Lobo – Lobo is so attuned to her emotional and physical state and picks up on everything. Whenever Lexi is processing and integrating a particular trauma during the session, Lobo can sense it and will move to the part of Lexi's body where she feels it, or will lie on her left or right side to support her.

Lexi, 40, is a teacher and therapist.

Lexi was diagnosed with a rare form of eye cancer when she was 14 months old. She spent her early years in and out of hospital and now has severely impaired vision.

During her sessions, she would flash back to operations when she was in hospital as a little girl. At other times, traumatic experiences she had had during childhood would surface, much of which she had blocked out. She did well at school, but was brought up to believe that she was not beautiful and that being a sexual being was in some way wrong.

Successful in her career, Lexi had a great social life and a loving husband, but one thing was missing: she desperately wanted to be a mum. They had been trying to conceive for 12 years, and although her doctor told her that there should be no complications, Lexi sensed that there were energetic blockages she was holding on to.

She takes up the story:

'My one-to-one sessions brought up traumatic memories that had been stored in my body without my knowledge. Within the safety of Rebecca's care, I was able to engage with these memories safely without experiencing distress or discomfort. The change in my moods, appearance, physicality and overall demeanour was tangible not just to me, but to everybody around me. I can only describe the work as life-changing and cannot recommend it highly enough.

'When I lay down and started the process, I had very strong

emotions coming up but at the same I felt safe. It was the first time in my life I had ever experienced anything like this.

'The preverbal trauma from my early childhood – things that I hadn't consciously processed – had left me in a constant state of anxiety to which I was oblivious. I was incredibly distressed about everything – being on public transport, even just lying in bed.

'I have always tended to steer clear of strong emotions, but being kept safe and grounded during the sessions as the flashbacks of severe trauma were coming through made all the difference.

'Afterwards, I felt a greater sense of wellbeing and less anxiety. I had to do a presentation in front of 200 people a few days later and I was able to stay more stable and grounded than I've ever felt before.

'At our one-on-one sessions, I explored different layers of strong physical sensations that I was feeling in my body. Every time, I could feel huge layers of trauma stripping away within my physical body, and also in terms of images and emotions in my body.

'I was kept with those sensations, so rather than escaping or being drawn into the drama of the experience, the tears, the anticipation of what might emerge, and the loss of centre, we would respond with sound or movement, and Rebecca would use words or acupressure to ensure these emotions were released.

'I have always been fiercely independent, but when leaving the sessions I noticed that people would come up and ask me if I needed help on the tube or finding a station. Previously I would always tell people that I was fine and I could do it myself, but I started feeling grateful for the help and accepting it. My energy was beginning to change and I was becoming less defensive. I felt more comfortable in my skin and wasn't trying to hide from the world.

'If challenges come up, I stick with the breath and the feeling and somehow emotions can move through me. It's as if I am allowing the body to not cling on to certain patterns or emotions but am giving them free flow energetically through the body.'

Lexi and I worked together for one year. She was able to release the fear and mistrust that her body had been holding on to and I'm thrilled to tell you that she now has a beautiful baby girl. Her breath pattern showed that she did not feel safe in her body, and when she started to feel safe, her body began to let go and trust that it was.

Some easy steps to establishing an open breath and understanding energetic blockages

Start in the belly

By inhaling in this way, the abdomen is pushed outwards, causing the diaphragm to extend downwards, opening up the lower part of our lungs. This is extremely beneficial since it is the area with the highest density of alveoli – the small air sacs that transfer oxygen into our bloodstream.

Come up into the midsection

Once it is fully in the abdomen, the breath wave moves across the diaphragm and up to the chest. It is within the diaphragm area that most restrictions are found. Known as the 'fear belt', this part of our body carries most of our emotional trauma and muscular tension from fight-or-flight responses.

It's very common to carry emotions like worry and anxiety in the tummy area. When we are excited, we feel 'butterflies in our stomach' or if we are nervous our 'tummy is in knots'. If people feel panicked, they might feel tightness just below the sternum in the solar plexus area, which is an energetic power point.

Move into the chest area

Once across the diaphragm, the breath wave travels up the chest and across the heart. The heart area is the second area that is often congested, mostly with tight muscular responses from repressed emotions such as loss, grief, love and ecstasy. We hold on to a lot of tension in the shoulders and upper chest. Often, when we feel stressed or are finding it hard to let go, these areas can feel very tight, which can lead to anxiety or panic attacks.

The throat area

Once past the heart area, the breath wave peaks into the upper chest and throat: the area of higher will. It is at the top of the breath wave that the secondary breathing muscles (sternocleidomastoid, trapezius and pectoralis minor) come into play. These secondary muscles provide balance and stability to our breathing system but, being much lighter than the primaries, they also tire more rapidly. When working with the throat area, we may have some blockages around communication and expression. Think about times when you are 'stuck for words', 'can't find the words' or you are 'holding your words back'. Another key place for holding tension is in the jaw, where repressed emotions of anger or grief can manifest in teeth grinding.

....

The breathwork truly helps you clear away stress and anxieties, both current and old. After just a few sessions, I felt invigorated, lighter and happier. I had asthma before starting Transformational Breath but now I no longer need to use my inhalers.

Maria, 35, mother of two

....

⊨═ EXERCISE ═⊨

RELAXING ASTHMATIC EXERCISE

The following exercise can be helpful in relaxing symptoms experienced by asthma sufferers. Try it on your own to gently begin to soften and relax the asthmatic breath pattern.

Sit on the ground and lean up against a wall – or you can lie on the floor, but make sure you are propped up by cushions so you are at a 45–75-degree angle.

Inhale a slow, deep breath through the nose. Place one or two fingers directly on the muscles just below the breastbone and apply gentle pressure so the muscles relax. This area might be a bit tender at first due to accumulated tension but it will feel better as it begins to relax.

Exhale freely, quickly and easily, as if you are releasing a big weight. Consciously ask your body to relax. Feel the upper chest relax as you release the breath.

Don't be discouraged if this doesn't happen immediately. Remember that you are working with years of unproductive patterning.

Repeat this for about five minutes while remaining soft and gentle in those muscles.

Relax completely while breathing in and out through the nose.

Nicola, 54, is a breathworker. This is her story.

Breathwork has been a life-changer and a lifesaver for me.

I started out of curiosity and soon realised how dysfunctional my breath was. I had sleep apnoea at night and I also used to hold my breath during the day when I was concentrating on something such as starting up my laptop. Practising breathwork remedied this and I found a free-flowing breath with relatively little practice, even when unconscious at night. My sleep apnoea vanished! I decided to sign up for training.

I could not have begun to imagine how much I would rely on the power of breathwork for my future healing. I was diagnosed with breast cancer and breathwork became an essential part of my coping strategy and recovery. As I underwent surgery, losing both of my breasts and hurtling headlong into chemotherapy, breathwork was always there to help me get through the physical pain and emotional struggle. There were days after chemotherapy when all I did for hours was focus on my breath and it became my saviour, guiding me to wellness.

The cancer took its toll, but the emotional turmoil reached a whole new level when my husband and I parted just as my treatment was coming to an end. We were not strong enough together to weather the storm. This is where the breathwork truly sustained and supported me. I have no idea where I would be now without it.

I feel like Houdini, freeing myself from the impossible emotional and physical knot of my situation. I found a deep spiritual practice through the breath and a confidence that no matter what, I would always be supported. It really has been my invaluable guide, there for me throughout my journey, on every level, taking me as deep as I needed to go, gently yet powerfully.

Emotions and Feelings

Emotion is energy-in-motion. Let's stop looking at emotion as being positive or negative but simply see it as energy.

Heavier energies can disrupt our lives when they stay with us. Disease causes chaos in the body and plays havoc with the mind, and although our body has an innate intelligence and is constantly sending messages to let us know when something is happening, often we miss the signs.

Emotion can be a record of our past living in the body. If the emotional body is living in the past, the unconscious mind believes it. We have been taught to resist and push away the things that don't feel good instead of actually feeling them and dealing with them, which can create negative feelings on a cellular level. Thoughts can be just as toxic as some of the things we consume and the breath helps us to release these toxins through our exhale.

Energy makes us move, it makes our light bulbs glow, but what is the relationship between physical matter and energy? Einstein's formula $E=mc^2$ shows a relationship between energy and matter. Matter can change into energy and energy can change into matter – the process doesn't only move in one direction. Sometimes we have a great deal of vitality and clarity of mind, whereas at other times we can feel distinctly lacking in energy.

The mind alters the flow of energy through the body, which in turn has an effect on the mind. William Walker Atkinson's illuminating book *Science of Breath* explains that when someone dies and the vital energy departs, we say the person has 'expired' and when someone experiences increased mental energy and creativity, we might describe that person as 'inspired'.

Some people find the idea of energy healing hard to comprehend, yet we have all experienced feelings of high, dense or low energy, high vibrations and low vibrations. At a music concert, fans collectively feel the energy bringing them into a higher state and leave feeling elated. Often people feel music is their church or spiritual source. When we sing in groups or are dancing in a club, the sound lifts and raises the vibration.

Sometimes we feel negativity in people and might say: 'You could cut the atmosphere with a knife.' A friend's energy might 'feel very negative' and leave you drained and zapped, while another individual will make people feel uplifted. We have all experienced the buzz when a person walks into the room and lights it up, transforming the atmosphere. This is the power that talented musicians and performers possess.

⊨ EXERCISE ⊨

WORKING THROUGH EMOTIONS WE WANT TO CONQUER

Here's a simple breathing technique for you if you're in a meeting and it's getting heated and you can feel your temperature rising or your heart beginning to pound, or you're feeling nervous walking into a room of people you haven't met before. Or maybe you are stuck in a traffic jam and you can feel yourself getting into a rage.

First take a deep breath and take a moment to notice the sensations in your body.

Notice where your breath is and how it feels.

Are your shoulders hunched, raised or tense? If so, take another deep breath in and let the exhale go, allowing the shoulders to relax.

What other sensations can you feel? Are there butterflies in your tummy or is it tense?

Gently breathe into your belly, notice the sensations and acknowledge them. Breathe in and on the exhale, let go of any tension being held here.

Notice your jaw: is it relaxed or clenched? Breathe in and out, letting go of any tension here.

Notice your body: is it leaning more to one side or are you holding part of your body in a particular way?

Continue to breathe into any area where you can feel tension or sensations.

What are you feeling? Is it anger, rage, fear, anxiety? Take another deep breath and rather than trying to push that feeling away, breathe into it and acknowledge it is there. Greet it like an old friend. 'Oh hello, anger, there you are! I can feel you,' and breathe through it.

Become the observer of the feeling, get interested. It's just an old pattern coming back to say hello.

Emotion is energy-in-motion. It's not good or bad. Rather than engaging with it, breathe deeply into it and by becoming the observer, you will become detached from it. Very gradually, this begins to fade away and the body can relax again.

I get nervous when I have to speak in front of large groups. In the past, this was something I wouldn't have been able to do at all, but now when I feel old familiar sensations coming up, I sit with them and breathe through them in this way. I become the observer and rather than try to push them away, I breathe. It takes practice, and some days it's more effective than others. What we are trying to achieve is not feeding the emotion or entertaining it but stepping outside, becoming the observer, and the breath is key to this.

Trusting your breath

When practising breath sessions, each day you will have a different experience. You cannot anticipate what will come up: you must leave that up to the breath and what is required that day.

Judy is 28 and works in law. She describes a breath session.

Can my body hear me? As I begin to connect to my inner breath and inwardly engage with my body, I can feel my tissues responding, my nervous system listening and sensations coming down my right arm within minutes. My tummy feels like there is something heavy on top, holding me down, pushing me into the Earth.

My mouth begins to tingle and my jaw feels tight. Rebecca asks me to make sound by toning and pounding the ground with my fists. Toning is when we make sound during the breath session in order to experience sound and its effects in other parts of the body. No words or melody, just the sound of one tone which helps to move towards inner balance. This feels strange at first but then I feel my breath open even more and all the cells in my body start responding. I let go of my mind and with each exhale I use the affirmation 'I let go, I let go.' My whole body starts vibrating and I feel my heart centre open with each inhale and exhale. The sound is very primal as I can feel all the cells in my body responding.

Turns out I didn't know how to let go of control. I was constantly setting myself up to fall. The sensations on my right side were indicating that my masculine side was going into overdrive to succeed, be the best and show the world I could be someone, but the breath in my tummy was not grounded and I wasn't present. I was too much in the future or the past.

Control = power but surrender = bliss. Each breath helped

me to rewire my thought patterns and begin to trust my feminine nature, my creativity and my nurturing side. I chose to let go and trust. The body breathes a sigh of relief. At last. She can hear me.

Harnessing energy

Our body is made up of conscious cells that experience emotion, and we can learn to openly connect to our body with compassion by understanding that concept. We can also alleviate and overcome pain and fear by engaging the breath with the body.

In her book *Everything You Need to Know to Feel Go(o)d*, Dr Candace Pert, a former chief of brain biochemistry at the US National Institute of Mental Health, asserts: 'As our feelings change, this mixture of peptides travels throughout your body and your brain. And they're literally changing the chemistry of every cell in your body.' Dr Pert helped to switch the paradigm from 'emotions as neuroscience' to 'emotions as biology'. Peptides are a group of compounds that behave as molecules of communication within our body. The neuropeptides in this case are molecules of communication for the brain cells (neurons).

When you hold on to your history, you do it at the expense of your destiny. So ask yourself this: are you willing to spend all that energy on where you have been, or would you rather spend that energy on where you are now?

How do you feel today?

When we ask people how they are, often they respond with 'I'm fine', 'I'm good', 'I'm really well, thanks', but is that how they really feel? We answer this way because we don't want to burden others with what may be going on in our lives.

In a perfect world, we want to feel happy, calm, focused, enthusiastic, open and positive (and being surrounded by like-minded people would be even better). When we are feeling stressed, negative or are experiencing low self-esteem, our energy gets consumed in self-preservation. We try to hide these feelings, not always successfully, becoming irritable or defensive, but it's not really how we want to be.

Human beings are masters of burying or hiding our emotions. When we feel inadequate, lonely, bored or are experiencing heartache, we try to escape these feelings. And even when we feel good, we want more rather than to stay content. Wouldn't it be more satisfying if we could learn to just sit and be with our feelings?

Trapped emotions can be buried so deep inside that we can't access them through speaking therapy, as we are unaware of them. Often we have blocked them out because they were too painful to deal with at the time. The breath allows us to hear them as they resurface from within. As a facilitator, I have learned to hear these trapped emotions, and everyone can learn to do this. Traumatic, hurtful events lead us to repress or suppress our emotions as a coping mechanism in order to fit in and be who we think we should be.

How we feel = how we breathe

How we feel emotionally directly affects our breathing. If we are feeling depressed, the breath is shallow, the body contracts, our shoulders are hunched and the head hangs low. If we are feeling happy and relaxed, our breath automatically feels freer.

Earlier, I explained how throughout life, we experience drama and trauma on a mental, emotional and physical level. We all have a story. Here follows a deeper description of what we may be holding on to.

When an individual experiences restriction or trauma, whether through a challenging birth, injury or emotional shock to the nervous system, the body alters its priority to survival mode. The sooner that trauma, shock and restriction are released from the body, the easier and faster the healing process becomes.

Birth

Our entry into the world is dramatic and miraculous at the same time. We spend 9 months cocooned in the safe environment of the womb, and on entering the world and taking our first breath, we are often met by loud voices and bright lights in a hospital delivery room. Generally, it takes a healthy newborn 10 seconds to take their first breath. It's a lot to take in, and the temperature of the room is no longer that of the cosy womb. Furthermore, if there are complications or anxieties being held by our mother, they can be transferred to us, and we may hold on to the trauma from birth. While we cannot remember these early events as our brains are still developing, our body and spirit can retain them.

Prue, 38, is a massage therapist. This is her story.

I first booked a treatment because I was pregnant with my second child. There had been complications when I'd given birth to my first child, and I was holding on to quite a bit of fear about giving birth again.

Although I had done hypnobirthing for my previous pregnancy, I wanted to do something that was one-on-one that would help with my breathing during labour. I had heard a lot about conscious breathwork, but I hadn't really explored it for myself. As a massage therapist and reflexologist, I would usually instinctively choose a body treatment, but in this instance, being pregnant seemed a good excuse to book a session.

My first treatment was mind-blowing. As soon as I met Rebecca I immediately trusted her. I usually hate feeling vulnerable or exposed, but any anxiety I had evaporated as soon as I walked into the clinic.

I had no idea what to expect, and I'd had no idea that through breathing my body could go into a trance. It's hard to find words to explain the depths that I went to during those treatments. Not only was I able to release stored negativity that was being held in my body, but I even felt that I connected to universal wisdom and received images and experienced connections that I really needed at that time.

I felt much more secure about giving birth and more connected to my unborn baby. Before the sessions I'd been very scared and anxious about the birth, but the breathwork definitely shifted that. I just felt *better*: more solid in myself. Breathing moved my state from fear of giving birth to confidence, so even though the birth didn't go quite as I wanted, I felt empowered enough to trust and just go with it. I firmly believe it would have been a more difficult experience without the breathwork.

Early childhood and adolescence

What may have been traumatic at the time for a small child is not necessarily an eternal or relevant memory for us now. Do you still remember the fear you experienced the first time you went to the dentist, or were barked at by a big scary dog? All sorts of firsts happen during this period: a teacher telling you off, a friend ditching you as their best friend, being bullied at school, having to stand up in front of your classmates and speak publicly, having your heart broken by your first love, your parents divorcing, and without necessarily realising that we are holding on to them still, these events can lead to feelings of neglect or abandonment in later life. We block out certain events that may have been too painful at the time.

The physical manifestation of emotions

Think about the times when you have felt emotion coursing through your body, when you hear a song you love or you are watching a mesmerising performance and can feel the hairs tingling on the back of your neck. When you are captured by a moment, it takes your breath away and gives you goose bumps.

If you're angry, you can feel tension in your jaw. If you're lost for words, your throat feels tight. And when you feel like you've been carrying the weight of the world on your shoulders, everything feels tense.

Do you remember the first time you fell in love and were floating on air, and the contrast between that elation and the despondency of having your heart broken and feeling so heavy with sadness that you wondered if you'd ever feel happy again?

Suppression and repression consume energy

It's a conscious choice to suppress emotions and not express or dwell on a particular thought or feeling. We choose this route because sometimes we just can't deal with them any other way. We acknowledge and accept their presence and the fact they may re-emerge, only to be suppressed again. Repressed emotions are different: we have buried them so deeply that we are not even aware they are there. It's the subconscious' way of protecting us.

When we can't let go of material in our subconscious mind, we are fighting internally to hold back that energy. Once it is released, we can experience a feeling of calm relief and feel lighter and freer. When we are willing to accept our emotions and feel them in our body, we can free ourselves.

The key here is not overthinking or analysing feelings and remembering that emotion is simply e-motion – energy and movement in our body – which sometimes gets stuck, making us feel heavy or drained. Forget the idea of an emotion being good or bad; try and simply experience it for what it is. It might feel uncomfortable at first but being present with our emotions has many rewards.

Breathing consciously is an effective way to transform energy. When you are in the grip of a reaction, you may notice your breathing is shallow or rapid, your throat gets tight, you can feel a pulsating sensation in your tummy or your solar plexus. Your face may get hot or your chest may start to tighten.

When you feel centred, happy or peaceful, you breathe with ease. One of the benefits of conscious breathing is to help you find your centre, or anchor, as I prefer to call it. That anchor is just below your belly button. When you feel off balance, try breathing deeply into this place and notice how you begin to feel more grounded. In fact, it is the easiest way to get centred when you find yourself being triggered by the words or behaviour of others.

Breathing can also help to halt the energy that goes into focusing on negative thoughts. When you breathe deeply, it can shift your energy from simply thinking to feeling more in touch with your body. Once you are more in touch with your body, you can move out of a reactionary state and into a place of deep inner knowing.

Sometimes in our careers, lifestyles or relationships, we can feel trapped by our emotions. By accepting them and not judging them, we give ourselves permission to achieve a greater balance in life. One thing I can guarantee is that being present with whatever is going on in your body will carry over into other aspects of your life.

The more we cultivate our inner strength and experience both comfortable and uncomfortable emotions, the more empowered we will be with who we are and the less dependent we become on things going right in life in order to feel good. The challenges don't disappear but during chaotic or uncertain times, our breath helps us through, revealing the beauty around us.

Alex is 35 and a musician. She describes her personal breathing practice.

I use my breathing practice every day, and when challenges arise, rather than go back into an old pattern or reaction, I breathe.

My breath is connected: my inhale and exhale have no pause in between and I can feel the breath inside me flowing in a circular motion like an ocean wave. I've been taken back to my story, the depths of despair, not knowing what the truth is, and I can't bear it, I don't want to be here anymore, I don't know how to find the answers, I am exhausted.

The breath picks me up and turns the story around the way night turns into day. I am able to step out of it and become the observer. The whole perspective of the story is turned around and at last I genuinely feel I can let go.

So much of this stuff is not mine and I energetically hand it back to who it belongs to. I continue to let go as tears pour from my eyes, but I am not crying: I am ecstatic. I feel free.

This breath in my body feels so powerful, yet I am making no effort. It feels as if the breath has taken over and is breathing itself. If the whole world could breathe like this it would be a very different place. We wouldn't be trying to escape our feelings; we would accept them all.

As I breathe, I feel my heart open and embrace a deep-rooted love connection – not sentimental love, but really deep love. Love is everything.

Dragging our feelings around

Many of the core feelings we suppress and repress come from fear. Fear comes in many layers including anger, sadness, guilt, embarrassment, shame and grief. Harbouring these feelings can turn them into bitterness or resentment.

Imagine if you saw a child carrying these feelings around in a large sack; how long would you expect them to hang on to them? We'd want to help that child let go of all that baggage, so why do we insist on carrying these feelings inside ourselves? By guarding the hurt inside us, we are hurting ourselves, and when those feelings are triggered, they lead us to hurt others as our shadow self comes out and reveals itself. Think of it as a serpent with many heads . . . every now and then, the jealous, resentful, bitter or angry head lashes out.

It might help to consider these feelings and emotions as children, or your child-self, trying to be heard. So when they arise, notice them, and when they come up through the breath, gently, without judgement, breathe into them. When we push these feelings away, we are just pushing them back down inside again, and instead of disappearing, they come back louder and louder until we hold them, listen to them and they begin to quieten.

Birds

Author and meditation teacher Jeff Foster makes an interesting analogy to help deal with thoughts, which resonates with me. (You can catch him on YouTube.)

Jeff says we should be aware that our thoughts may never go away. Urging them to leave your head is not helpful. Think of them as birds singing, 'I'm a success', 'I'm a failure.' They are different songs but each bird has the right to an opinion and the right to sing. It's a democracy.

Instead of willing the bird to disappear, try instead to make friends with it, and you'll realise it's just a sound, a thought. There are also different birds singing different songs, questions that demand answers – where to go, what to do, which voice to listen to, how to avoid falling apart – and some of them are louder and others are quieter. But they are just birds, and the more you pay attention to them, the louder they'll get. 'I'm a fraud, they aren't going to believe me, what do I know about the breath? I'm a failure, I'm worthless.'

These are old thoughts. We all have them, even if we don't admit it. It's still taboo to talk openly about this kind of thing. If you went to a dinner party and someone asked how you were and you retorted with 'Well, I have this thought that I'm a loser and a failure', your fellow diner would lose interest in you very quickly. So we are conditioned not to vocalise these thoughts.

It's very liberating to realise that your thoughts don't define you. These birds are allowed to sing their song, so don't judge them, but acknowledge them and the fact that what they are singing is not personal, it's not the truth, it's not really you.

Creating space in the mind

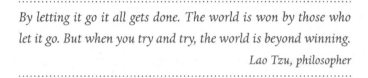

By letting it go it all gets done. The world is won by those who let it go. But when you try and try, the world is beyond winning.

Lao Tzu, philosopher

Often we spend a lot of time in our thoughts and sometimes experience recurring negative thought patterns. Don't believe everything your mind is telling you; sometimes it can be very destructive. Here's a very simple exercise to help let go of the mind clutter to create room for clarity and calm. Firstly, leave all your thoughts at the door. Whatever it is you have to do today or tomorrow or should have done and haven't managed to yet, leave it all at the door. You can return to it later.

⊨ EXERCISE ⊨

Close your eyes and sit up straight.

Feel the ground beneath your feet and your sitting bones on the seat beneath you.

Relax your shoulders and let out a deep sigh.

Begin to notice the breath and become aware of the inhale and the exhale.

Imagine the breath coming in and out like a wave.

Breathe softly and deeply in through the nose and out through the nose with a little pause in between.

As you inhale, guide the breath into the belly, encouraging a deep diaphragmatic breath.

Allow the mind to wander to the breath, and each time you notice you're going back into your thoughts, take your mind back to the breath.

Begin to draw your focus and attention to the rise and fall of your breath.

Allow the breath to flow. No forcing it or pushing it. Gentle breathing.

Expand your awareness inside and let go of the outside.

There is nowhere to go, nothing to do, just stay present with your breath.

Everything is as it should be right now, there is no wrong and there is no right.

Stay present with your inhale and your exhale.

Notice any thoughts that are there not pushing them away, just taking the focus to the breath. Deepen your breath connection, by listening, observing the breath and the thoughts should naturally become more distant and quieter.

Step outside of the thoughts and observe them.

Not entertaining them. Just allowing them to pass like clouds in the sky.

Breathe in and breathe out, letting go of anything that no longer serves you.

Exhale away any tension or worries.

Inhale in new energy, positivity and light.

Letting go of the pull of the future and the pull of the past.

Continue to go deeper inside, explore and expand your awareness inside with each breath.

Staying in this moment which is NOW.

Keep practising this for 2–3 minutes and then notice how your mind feels.

Mirror projection

When people make us angry or upset or we don't like something we see in them, it's usually a reflection of something we don't like in ourselves, like looking into a mirror. I have learned to be really grateful to these messengers, as painful as it might be at the time.

When I reflect back to before I had discovered breathwork and was taking medication, I was putting a plaster on my thoughts and feelings to stop them leaking out and keep control of them. The breath allows us to feel them, accept them and integrate them. Sometimes it's not pretty, but in order to grow, we need to accept every side of ourselves.

Being vulnerable is fine too, and when I see people sharing their vulnerability, the first thing I think is how brave they are. People can connect and empathise with that, and it's powerful and beautiful to witness. As inspirational author and speaker Brené Brown says: 'Vulnerability sounds like truth and feels like courage. Truth and courage aren't always comfortable, but they're never weakness.'

Stop giving yourself such a hard time

Even the most powerful, successful people on this planet have insecurities. My definition of power and success is to be able to let go of the search and be happy with what we have as opposed to striving for what we think we're lacking. Feeling balanced inside should be the ultimate goal.

Unfortunately, we can't help but compare ourselves to others, imagining they have a better life, a more fulfilling career or a more understanding partner, yet we are projecting our judgements about ourselves onto others. It's a myth that material wealth creates happiness. Some of the wealthiest people I have worked with are the unhappiest and some of the happiest people I have met, whose presence lights up a room, are in poverty but are grateful for what they do have.

Author and renowned shaman Sandra Ingerman explains this beautifully:

I have never seen a group of people comparing the stars in the night sky. Nor have I heard people comparing the beauty of flowers. We might feel drawn to one flower over another, but we honour all flowers for the beauty they possess. We must treat one another – and ourselves – the same way.

So what do we fear?

We fear not being good enough, not being someone, not being loved, rejection, not being accepted, loneliness, letting people down, being taken advantage of. Everyone else seems to have it all worked out so why don't we? We are here on this planet just one time and that goes pretty quickly. Relax: all you can do is be the best you can be and that is enough. And if you haven't been the best you can be today, there is always tomorrow.

Breathing through the fear

Breathing through our fear creates more room for flexibility and acceptance. Fearing the unknown and resisting it takes a lot of energy, so if we can breathe into what is actually happening, we allow the energy to flow.

We don't have to like everything that is happening, but resistance is fear-based and accompanied by negative emotions such as anger, judgement, resentment and blame. It can cause depression and anxiety, negating inspiration, enthusiasm and zest for life.

From an early age, we are conditioned to perform. Babies arrive in the world with unique personalities and view the world from their own perspective, letting you know when they are hungry, tired or frustrated. The world is about them and their parents feed them, clothe them and cuddle them.

Around the age of three, we begin to notice what makes people happy, sad, laugh, angry or fearful, and discover how to get attention. Our social circle widens to include friends at nursery and then school, and we slot into the dynamics of the new scenarios.

The key stage of emotional development takes place between the ages of three and seven years old, when we start being conditioned by parents, culture, society and religion about who we are, how we look at others, and how we relate to the world. This affects how we perceive and what we think is possible.

We label ourselves the clown, the entertainer, the people-pleaser, the black sheep, the victim, the co-dependent, the leader, the perfectionist – maybe we are all of these in different settings. These memories and thoughts are stored in our subconscious and our cells like on a computer hard drive. The breath helps us to release and clear them, so we can undo these labels and discover who we always have been in the first place.

Breathing through fear

The only thing we have to fear is fear itself.

Franklin D. Roosevelt

Fear is a very old pattern and often it stops us in our tracks. Fear of failure can affect our whole life and hold us back from doing what we love or trying something new. Our body can sense it before we can; it tenses up and our breathing pattern changes. We can feel it reacting in our body, and by remembering that it is simply energy we can take hold of it and alter the feeling, rather than it taking hold of us. Here's a simple exercise to notice the pattern, breathe through it and come out the other side.

Try this if you are experiencing fear. Reframe the story and remember it's just a story. It's not real.

⊨ EXERCISE ⊨

First, be aware of the feelings and sensations that you are feeling in your body.

Track them and get curious: is it in your belly, is it in your chest, or perhaps somewhere else?

Notice your breathing pattern: is it rapid, is it shallow, does it feel restricted?

Now breathe deeply using the diaphragm. Allow the belly and rib cage to expand as you inhale and contract as you exhale.

Notice the feelings and greet them like old friends. Become the observer rather than entertaining the feelings and feeding them.

Feel your feet on the ground and imagine that they are growing roots.

Root down to power up.

As you breathe in and out, imagine the breath coming all the way down to your feet.

Be aware of the sensations in your body as you breathe in and breathe out.

Try not to fight the sensations or push them away, just notice them.

Breathe through the sensations in your body as you breathe in and out.

Breathe in love: where there is love there cannot be fear. Use the affirmation 'I let go.'

Continue to breathe deeply into the belly, inhaling and exhaling, and stay present with your breath.

This will help to ground and centre you, bringing you back to the present moment.

Strong men do cry

Why do we apologise for crying? My clients are often surprised by their emotions resurfacing, and although society is making it more acceptable for men to cry and express sensitive feelings, our Western culture still sends the message that 'strong men don't cry'. On an ancestral level, it is ingrained in many men that masculine identity means holding back the tears.

A little boy may wear his emotions on his sleeve, and while it is natural for a child to have a tantrum, to stop in the middle of combat and have a good cry, in an adult this would be seen as inappropriate. There is an expectation for men and women in the world of business to store these emotions away and wear a mask at the office. Over time, repressed emotions can trigger physiological changes that manifest in clinical symptoms such as high blood pressure and post-traumatic stress disorder.

Forget appearing over-emotional; it's healthy to rush off to the loo and have a good cry, whether they are tears of rage, sadness, frustration or exhaustion. It takes great effort and energy to fake or hide emotions, and that can cause huge mental stress. Tears are cleansing and help to shed hormones and toxins that build up through stress. Studies suggest that crying stimulates the production of endorphins, our body's natural painkiller and feel-good hormone.

I had the pleasure of working with an inspiring group of young men who asked if I would hold group workshops for them. Having been friends for a long time, the bond between them was evident, and it was beautiful to witness their honesty and openness. They were unafraid to be vulnerable and share their true feelings and experiences at the end of each session. At a time when official figures show that male suicide rates are more than three times higher than the rate for females, it's important to share the fact that breathwork is unique in offering people help when they may find it hard to express in words what they are holding on to. It's especially helpful for men who have been conditioned to shut down emotionally from an early age. I am grateful and honoured to have had the opportunity to work with this particular group. They taught me so much, and it gives me hope that there is a new generation of men exploring these ideas and supporting each other.

Dan, 25, is an entrepreneur. This is his story.

I first came to a breathing session to seek a powerful experience that could connect me with long-lasting happiness, after reading glowing reviews about the power of this method.

I had a long history of depression and self-defeating behaviours due to an abusive childhood. I tried yoga, meditation, the Chinese breathing therapy neigung and traditional therapy in a bid to end my suffering, and while they had positive effects, they felt too slow to offer any real comfort during my early 20s.

I was enjoying professional success at a young age but I felt even more empty and lost at finding no peace or long-lasting happiness in any 'success' I had achieved.

Within 5 minutes of my first group session, everything shifted in a very powerful and completely unexpected way. Suddenly, the pain I was running from was manageable, and I felt a type of peace that can't be put into words. It was a spiritual experience.

Beyond the inner peace on a physiological level, there was an aliveness that overcomes your body while it is 'breathing'. New sensations come up, your body moves of its own accord, and you feel your energy in a real, undeniable and pleasurable sense.

As my body surrendered, I felt many years' worth of trapped emotions and tears leaving me. I felt like a wounded child who was finally being cared for and safe in the world, a feeling I had not experienced in my childhood.

Breathwork enabled me to grieve for my childhood, heal and move on. I'm confident this would not have happened any other way. I continue to practise – not as often as I would like, but enough to keep me in a healthy and positive place, and for that I am eternally grateful.

React or respond?

Often we react to situations as opposed to responding to them. Holidays or big events bring family and friends together to celebrate, but we notice we may fall back into old patterns, dynamics and roles. We can be triggered by our family, work colleagues, lovers or children, and unconsciously we can find ourselves reacting to certain situations, events or people in old, familiar ways that echo the past.

Sigmund Freud identified this pattern as repetition compulsion, an attempt of the unconscious to replay what's unresolved so we can 'get it right'. Carl Jung also believed that what remains unconscious does not dissolve, but rather resurfaces. In other words, we tend to repeat our unconscious pattern until we bring it into the light of awareness. Both Freud and Jung noted that whatever is too difficult to process does not fade away on its own, but is stored in our unconscious.

When we trigger each other in relationships, work or everyday life, it's an opportunity for integration. Our breath is longing to make itself known, and the voices we suppress and push down want to be heard. Breath is a shapeshifter and will use our entire emotional and somatic landscape to bring us to life and remind us what it is to be here fully, open and present.

This can make us feel more vulnerable, but ultimately, when we release our mind and listen to the wisdom and intimacy of our heart, we can accept who we are and let go of the patterns that don't serve us.

Michelle, 34, is an occupational health therapist. This is her story.

I was introduced to Transformational Breath through a mutual friend who thought it might be beneficial – and she was right.

At the start of the first session, I was harbouring a significant amount of inner turmoil, anger, frustration and disappointment towards certain relationships, particularly with my sister and an old friend from university.

These feelings had been submerged for years, and instead of trying to resolve them, I continued to bury them. Upset and hurt by my sister or my friend, I tried to please them by placating them, 'forgiving' them, taking the blame or trying to fix their problems. In trying to make them happy, I ended up feeling disappointed and unappreciated.

A few years ago, my father and a close friend died unexpectedly, a few weeks apart. Then, after years of trying to conceive, in a complete state of grief, I found out I was pregnant. I struggled with being happy and sad at the same time. Feeling I'd emotionally imploded, I distanced myself from anyone who upset or hurt me, offering no explanation to the people around me.

This was particularly hard on my sister and my family, who

did not understand that their frustrations with my behaviour only alienated me further.

My first session affected me hugely. Returning home to my husband, I told him how I was feeling openly and honestly – something I had not been able to do for a long time. The session was so much harder than I had imagined, and mastering the breathing technique felt uncomfortable to me. I struggled to breathe, needing to stop, cough, feeling desperate for water.

As I listened to Rebecca's affirmations, alongside the gentle music and her encouragement to remember to breathe, I began to feel light-headed and my thoughts and feelings felt exposed. I struggled to breathe, holding my breath (something I do when I feel vulnerable), but she supported me to breathe through it. At the end of the session, I cried and felt strangely elated. There was a sudden outpouring of sadness mixed with hope. I experienced a strong sense that my father was sitting next to me, telling me, 'Everything will be okay. Just keep breathing.'

Breathwork continued to be challenging but I began to recognise internal blockages that prevented me from breathing freely – mostly anger and disappointment. With support, I tried to breathe through them. I made progress and began to understand more about myself and feel more receptive and open than I had for a long time.

In each session, specific affirmations washed over me, but as the sessions progressed, they started to resonate and I learned to have faith in them. Memories of incidents that, as a child, I had locked away and had affected my development flooded back.

I felt I had permission to untangle my emotional turmoil and view issues from a more mature perspective, instead of reverting to my childhood instincts. The physical sensations seemed to move up through my body after each session – travelling inwards and upwards from my feet and hands. On reflection, this was the start of my energy beginning to flow more freely around my body, unblocking my emotional baggage.

The breathwork highlighted the growing tensions in my relationship with my mother, and I believe that had I not been practising Transformational Breath, my relationship with her would have ended negatively.

I continue to practise and it helps enormously, offering me an outlet to set an agenda – something I struggled with at the start of my journey. Just 5 to 10 minutes makes me feel at peace, and while my life is not perfect, I am more confident in who I am and have a positive mechanism to effectively manage my life.

Mind and Body

....

Change needs to occur simultaneously in all three aspects – body, mind, and emotions – resulting in a new state of being for which there is no price.

Max Strom, writer and teacher

....

We now understand that breathing heals on many levels. The breath is the bridge linking our mind and body. The practice of deep breathing helps to stimulate our para-sympathetic nervous system (PNS), bringing us to a calm state. Diaphragmatic breathing stimulates the PNS, which allows the body to rest and digest, slowing the heart rate, lowering blood pressure and respiratory rate, and diverting the blood supply towards the digestive and reproductive systems.

When the PNS is active, the sympathetic nervous system (SNS) becomes less active – they counteract each other. The SNS raises heart rate, blood pressure and respiratory rate, diverting blood to the brain and skeletal muscle in readiness for fight or flight.

By deactivating or overriding the SNS, we can inter-rupt the cycle of adrenaline and cortisol production, which contribute to chronic stress levels and predispose us to panic attacks and anxiety.

It's possible, therefore, by voluntarily changing the rate, depth and pattern of breathing, to change the messages being sent from the body's respiratory system to the brain. Breathing techniques may provide a portal to the autonomic communication network, enabling us to make a change in our breathing patterns. This suggests we can send specific messages to the brain using the language of the body, a language the brain understands and responds to.

In their book *The Healing Power of the Breath*, Richard P. Brown and Patricia L. Gerbarg describe how messages from the respiratory system have rapid, powerful effects on major brain centres involved in thought, emotion and behaviour.

When breathing deeply, the diaphragm contracts downwards, creating negative pressure in the chest (the thoracic cavity), which draws air into the lungs, expanding the chest. The intercostal muscles and the muscles of the neck, back and shoulder blades contract when triggered to do so by behaviour or by increased respiratory demands.

We've established that emotional or mental upset may correlate to breathing restrictions. It is common to observe a change in our breathing pattern or the tendency to hold our breath as a reaction to feelings that overwhelm us. Often we are stuck living in the future or in the past, thinking of the things that we don't have and comparing our lives and ourselves to others. By becoming aware of our breathing, we can create balance and calm within the systems, thereby controlling levels of stress before they take control of us.

....

Maybe it's about unbecoming everything that we have become so we can be who we were in the first place.

Unknown

....

⊱═ EXERCISE ═⊰

SENDING GRATITUDE TO OUR BODY

You can do this either lying down or sitting up. Soften your focus and feel the ground beneath you. Allow your whole body to let go and relax: your neck, your back, your legs.

Take a slow deep breath in and let the exhale go with a big sigh, beginning to release any tension you may be holding onto in your body.

Imagine a beautiful white healing light coming in through the top of your head and filling your body. Feel it entering all the cells of your body and nourishing every part of you. Send a message thanking all the cells in your body.

Now take a deep inhale, breathing into all the tiny little muscles around your eyes, mouth and face, releasing any tension being held here.

Breathe into your neck and shoulders and feel yourself letting go of any tension being held here on the exhale. Breathe into your arms and your forearms, your wrists, your hands and your fingers. With each breath, send gratitude to all these parts of your body, imagining this beautiful white healing light filling these parts of you.

Now breathe into your chest and your rib cage. Take a deep

breath here and into your heart area and thank your heart for beating every day and every night. Let it know that you will treat it with great tenderness and care.

Breathe into all the organs in your body, every vein, bone and muscle, and imagine this beautiful iridescent white light filling every part of you. Send gratitude into all these parts of your body.

Imagine the breath creating space in your belly, your hips and your thighs, sending gratitude with each breath. The white healing light is flooding down and coming into your legs, knees, calves, feet and toes. Breathe in this white light and feel the energy and healing power of your breath. Each breath fills you with love for your body, sending gratitude.

Breathe into the whole of your body using the affirmation 'I arrive in my body', and when breathing out, affirm: 'I am home.'

Your body is your first home: Breathing in, I arrive in my body. Breathing out, I am home.

> *Thich Nhat Hanh, spiritual leader and peace activist*

Celebrate and love your body . . . it's a living miracle!

We all get hung up on how we look and give our bodies a hard time. The internal critic counting how many wrinkles we have, noticing too many rolls around the waistline and wishing for smaller hips and toned arms has a lot to answer for.

It's only when things go wrong that we recognise just how incredible our body is. Exercising, eating healthy foods, breathing consciously and sending gratitude are all ways to signify to our body that we want to give it a helping hand.

The emotional highway

The vagus nerve – the longest nerve in the torso, also known as 'the wanderer' – conducts messages between the brain and the internal organs in the body. Described as the 'super-highway nerve', a great deal of research is currently being carried out on this rather fascinating cranial nerve.

When we are under high levels of stress, the sympathetic nervous system activates into fight-or-flight mode, and our heart and respiration rates speed up. By breathing deeply, we help to trigger the parasympathetic nervous system to bring us back into a more relaxed state. Each time we breathe in and breathe out, we are sending different messages via the vagus nerve to the brain. The vagus nerve directly innovates the diaphragm into action and carries PNS and SNS fibres that feed back into the autonomic nervous system.

Dr Philippa Wheble, a GP, Transformational Breath therapist and researcher, says:

In the same way that we learn and evolve, our breathing pattern is shaped and altered by our experiences. Fear, shame, stress, guilt and loneliness all leave a footprint in our breath and influence how we react and respond to stress as we move through life.

If we accept these 'scars' and choose to change our breathing patterns through mindful practice, we open up to the possibility that changing our breathing pattern could change how we experience everything. Practising skills to observe our breathing without judgement and to adjust it in response to changing conditions can be extremely empowering. Our breath is a powerful tool for wellbeing and resilience which could help anyone who is experiencing stress, anxiety, low mood, ill health or grief.

There has been scientific attention on the connection between breathing, mental health and wellbeing for over 35 years. We simply do not understand the complex interplay between the breath, the body and the mind – except to say that there *is* a connection.

I believe in science and medicine. As doctors, we work in all shades of grey. We interpret and communicate evidence and patterns and balance risks and benefits. There are so many things that we don't know – we simply don't have the science yet. But if medicine has taught me anything, it's this: even if we do everything perfectly, there are no guarantees.

Conscious breathing is a powerful resource for personal resilience and wellbeing. It is a simple breathing practice which focuses mindful attention to yourself and your body and creates deep acceptance. I have no doubt that it would be an empowering and supportive adjunct to many treatment regimens and a powerful resilience tool for people who work in health and social care.

Gratitude is good for our health

Practising gratitude and positive thinking sends messages to our brain via neurotransmitters to the neural pathways.

Hebb's rule states that neurons that learn together fire quicker and wire together. The more times these neural pathways are activated, the less time it takes to stimulate the pathway for the neurons to wire together. If we keep feeding our brain negative thoughts, the neural pathways for negative thinking become stimulated.

I said earlier that when we connect to our breath and consciously breathe, it's like taking the mind to the gym. We can switch the mind's thought pattern by listening to our body and aiding our innately designed systems through our breath.

It takes practice, and some days it'll work better than others. The important thing is not to let it feel like a chore. If you just practise these exercises for 5–10 minutes a day, I promise you will notice a difference. And don't stress if you miss a day, as the aim here is not to beat yourself up but allow it to become a natural slice of your daily routine.

⊨ EXERCISE ⊨

GRATITUDE EXERCISE

This takes just 2 minutes, so try doing it every day for a week. You can do it anywhere – in bed before you get up, in the shower, on the train or during your break at work. If you want to get the most out of it, keep a notebook handy to jot down what you are grateful for. Put time and effort into your gratitude journal or keep a gratitude jar: write on a scrap of paper what you are grateful for and put it in the jar. Try to write one or two every day. See how you feel by the end of the week and carry that positive energy with you.

Breathe consciously in and out 10 times and repeat this set 3 times. Breathe in through the nose and out through the nose. Make a long inhale and a little pause followed by a relaxed exhale. Feel the belly and rib cage expand as you inhale and contract as you exhale.

As you breathe in, close your eyes and focus on 3 things you are grateful for. Maybe your friends, the air we breathe, the sea, the forests, or something wonderful like a child's smile or a hug from someone you love. You might want to thank your body for all its incredible systems that are working every day for you. Keep your focus there.

As you breathe in and out, feel life and energy coming into your body, healing your body, filling your cells and every part of your being. Stay with the rhythm of your breath, focus on each inhale and exhale and allow your breath to flow.

Now feel that energy coming into all the people around you and the people you love. Feel them being healed and having the life they deserve.

$$\vdash\!\!=\!\!=\!\!\dashv$$

The muscle of the soul

The psoas major, which I mentioned earlier, is a deep-seated core muscle, and some say it's the muscle of the soul. Originating from the lumbar vertebrae, it forms a strip of muscle along each side of the spine. Teacher and author of *Core Awareness* Liz Koch explains that our psoas muscles can be stressed and constricted from a young age:

> This situation is exacerbated by many things in our modern lifestyle, from car seats to constrictive clothing, from chairs to shoes that distort our posture, curtail our natural movements and further constrict our psoas.
>
> The lifelong chronic stress that is put on the psoas can lead to back, hip or knee pain, as well as digestive issues and dysfunctional breathing. In short, this muscle deserves our attention, a healthy psoas is an important ingredient for emotional wellness and physical health.
>
> Whether you suffer from a sore back or anxiety, knee problems or exhaustion, there's a good chance that constricted psoas might be contributing to your woes.

Since the psoas is closely linked to our fight-or-flight

mechanism, fear can be over-represented in those with constricted psoas. By restoring balance through the breath to your psoas muscles, you can release any pent-up tension and experience a profound effect, thus improving your physical and mental wellbeing.

The aim is to feel a greater sense of inner peace, along with fewer muscle aches and strains. There are many different exercises using the breath that you can employ to help release this: yoga, Nordic walking, stretching and core walking are just a few. If you have any injuries, find a teacher who can help you with some simple exercises and get you in the right postures so that you don't injure yourself further. The psoas major connects the upper body to the lower body, linking the breath to movement, feelings, energy and healing.

Here are some very simple exercises to help you release the psoas.

⊨ EXERCISE ⊨

PSOAS-RELEASING EXERCISE (ADAPTED FROM *THE VITAL PSOAS MUSCLE* BY JO ANN STAUGAARD-JONES)

The psoas is often overworked so core exercises can help this muscle.

Side bending
You can do this sitting or standing. Stand with feet

shoulder-width apart, body upright and arms overhead. Clasp the hands together. Keep the body upright and bend to the left and then bend to the right. With each bend, inhale and come back to the centre with an exhale.

Rising stomach stretch

Lie face down and bring the hands close to the shoulders. Engage the abdominals so as not to injure the lower spine. Keep the hips on the ground, look forward, and rise up by straightening the arms. If there is back pain, do not straighten the arms completely, and always press the shoulders down away from the ears. Repeat this 5 to 10 times, and remember to breathe.

Lunges (runner's stretch)

All variations of lunges are good for releasing the psoas. Begin standing with the left foot forward and the right leg back. Bend the front knee until it is directly over the toes, and slide the right leg straight back until it is parallel to the floor, if possible. Keep the feet forward and do not let the front knee go further forward than the toes. The spine is straight and the hands can rest on the hips or the fronts of the thighs. The hip flexors are strengthening in the front leg and stretching in the back leg. Hold for approximately 15 seconds, then repeat on the other side.

You can begin with 10 lunges on each side and build this up each day by adding 5 more. Remember to focus on the breath with each lunge, working slowly and methodically.

Making friends with stress

It is a scientific fact that stress creates reactions in the body that affect our physical, mental and emotional responses. Stress comes from our environment, our body and our thoughts. It is an inevitable and perfectly normal ingredient in our lives and isn't necessarily a bad thing.

Stress can be positive, keeping us alert and ready to avoid danger. It helps us to get the job done and only becomes negative when we face continuous challenges without relief or relaxation in between. As a result, we become overworked and stress-related tension starts to build.

Adrenaline is the primary fight-or-flight hormone and is largely responsible for the immediate reaction that happens when we are stressed. Imagine you are being chased by a fierce dog. Your heart pounds, your breathing gets faster, you might break into a sweat or your muscles might tense up. A frightening stimulus triggers a cascade of hormones in the brain, which results in adrenaline and cortisol being released. The adrenaline increases heart rate, blood pressure, respiratory rate, and diverts blood to the brain – making you more alert – and prepares the skeletal muscles for fight or flight.

Adrenaline also causes you to sweat (to manage the heat created by the muscles working hard) and contracts the pupils to sharpen your vision. Cortisol actually causes glucose to be released from glycogen stores, which is what gives you the surge of energy that is needed for fight or flight.

I'll let Amit Sood, Professor of Medicine at the Mayo Clinic College of Medicine, explain:

> The part of the brain which is responsible for emotions and survival instincts sends a message to the brain to produce corticotropin-releasing hormone (CRH). CRH then tells the pituitary gland which tells the adrenal glands to produce cortisol.
>
> When you remain in a heightened state of anxiety the body continuously releases cortisol. Too much cortisol can become toxic, increasing blood pressure.

In his book *Ageless Body, Timeless Mind*, author Deepak Chopra writes powerfully about the impact of stress hormones. He says:

> Our cells are constantly eavesdropping on our thoughts and being changed by them. A bout of depression can wreak havoc with the immune system; falling in love can boost it. Despair and hopelessness raise the risk of heart attacks and cancer, thereby shortening life. Joy and fulfilment keep us healthy and extend life. This means that the line between biology and psychology can't really be drawn with any certainty. A remembered stress, which is only a wisp of thought, releases the same flood of destructive hormones as the stress itself.

Ana, 36, is a neuroscientist. This is her story.

I came to Transformational Breath almost on a whim, without a clear understanding of what was involved. I'd been looking for a bodywork practitioner to help me with my posture, and two specialists mentioned that I had a very shallow breathing pattern and that it would be worthwhile to work on deepening my breathing.

I practised yoga and meditation but my breathing felt constricted, and during meditation I was aware of a tightness in my chest that I could not relieve. My goal was to try and move my breath down from the top of my lungs into my abdomen and loosen the tightness in my chest. I wasn't expecting the breathwork to have a profound impact on my life.

I had a difficult childhood, and had had therapy, which convinced me that I had dealt with my past issues. I did wonder if the lingering tightness in my chest might be some lasting childhood issues that were still unresolved.

I am a physician and scientist and my area of expertise is the brain. I also believe in the wisdom and efficacy of ancient or Eastern medicine for healing and preventing illness. Throughout my career, it was always understood that the brain influences the body, but it was not necessarily recognised that the body could affect the brain. Scientists have only recently begun to understand how significantly the way we move and breathe can affect the brain.

My first private session was incredibly intense. I came in very calm, expecting to learn some relaxing deep breathing against a soothing background of candles and incense. As I lay down and started the breathing technique, I began to cry. I am not moved to tears easily and am uncomfortable when I feel out of control or overly emotional.

I continued through the practice crying and sobbing, and the whole thing was very difficult. I found it hard to find a rhythm. I felt drained and confused as to what had happened. I was light-headed for a few days and noises seemed especially loud. My sleep seemed deeper than usual.

After a couple more sessions, I began to feel comfortable with the rhythm of breathwork, although I struggled to complete even 5 or 10 minutes of it by myself at home. However, by my fifth session, the breathing began to feel more natural.

Music helps me to relax into the breathing and I usually listen to *Chakra Chants* by Jonathan Goldman. When I do Transformational Breath before meditation, I feel more focused and able to settle into the meditation. I can now practise for longer periods of time, and the tightness in my chest is finally gone. If I have trouble sleeping, I'll do 10 minutes of breathing followed by a few minutes of meditation, and then am always able to sleep.

I find it hard to believe that breathing practice could have such a significant effect on my life, but it has. Unhappy in my field of practice, I left medicine several years ago to raise my children. I have started lecturing and am embarking on a second exciting career. I speak up for myself more now and feel more confident in my decisions.

Scientists are just beginning to appreciate the significant effect that the autonomous nervous system (sympathetic/parasympathetic nervous systems) has on the brain. This is currently a major area of research.

Letting Go

We have just one life on this amazing planet. We can either spend years dwelling on the past or the future, or we can live in the moment, forgive ourselves, and find compassion for those who have hurt us. It's a simple choice – we can carry that hurt or resentment inside us or we can choose to let it go. We have a choice. I'm not saying we shouldn't grieve for what we have lost (we will get to that part soon).

The world is changing and we are changing within it. Sometimes we have to set ourselves free from the toxic people in our lives or let go of lifestyles that no longer serve us. That friend who always makes you feel bad about yourself, the lover who is never going to commit, the person you thought you should be by now: losing old habits can feel like leaving old friends. We feel like part of us is missing for a while, but when we manage to let go, we will eventually realise why we had to, or indeed, why people had to let *us* go. I can't deny it hurts sometimes.

Daily, the body is breathing itself. We do not need to do anything, since, moment by moment, the breath continues, but when we start to make a choice about how we breathe, this filters and changes our perception of ourselves in this life. Our vision becomes less clouded, clearer.

Connecting to historic emotions we're still holding on to is key – the insecure thoughts, past hurts, regrets, heartbreaks, our parents' worries, our grandparents' conditioning and anxieties – we hold on to these things on energetic and ancestral levels.

The breath hears all of this. It rises and listens when we make a choice to connect to it. Sometimes we are holding on to these emotions so closely we don't even realise it, and if we do, we have no idea how to let them go. But once we learn to let go of the weightiness, we begin to feel lighter, we are floating on air, breathing away old stories and allowing those feelings of sadness and grief to come to the surface and be held and heard so we can truly heal ourselves.

My work with Bryan illustrates this. A champion boxer, Bryan first came to see me when he was preparing for a big title fight. When I start working with someone, I never know what is going to happen. I am not there to fix them, and they are the ones doing the work, always.

I don't engage with the left side of my brain, the analytical and logical side; I work with my right side, my intuition, senses and feelings. Breathwork is like a dance that flows, and quite simply, I hold a space and stay present. To witness long-held emotion leaving the body always confirms to me the power of our breath and how much I trust it.

Each time I facilitate people, they always remind me how brave we are as human beings and how we should never judge a book by its cover. Showing our vulnerability is one of the most powerful and authentic things we can do.

Back to Bryan. He didn't win the fight. He considered retiring, but something inside him was pushing him forward, so he decided to go back into training and compete in one more fight. Guess what: he won and got his title back. He decided to retire after his triumph.

Bryan, 35, is a professional light middleweight champion boxer. This is his story.

I first came for a breathing session thinking it would benefit my training and psychology. I've always wanted to be the best I can be in life, not just in boxing but for myself, my wife and my daughters. I've tried to give myself the best chance in life and make a success of it.

My breathing was very shallow, and as a result of that I'd been doing a lot of research on breathing and was already using hypnosis and listening to different meditation techniques.

I started martial arts at a young age before getting into boxing, and began competing professionally in kickboxing and boxing. This is where I faced all my fears. I enjoyed hitting punch bags as it relieved stress, and it also gave me a confidence I had never experienced before.

I've always been a survivor, but I had social anxiety from a young age and felt uncomfortable around other people. Boxing seemed to make me tougher when dealing with that negative emotion. There was an inner drive pushing me to do this.

I didn't have the greatest childhood and I don't have happy memories of being a kid. I realised that I was holding on to stuff on a subconscious level that I didn't know how to access.

The first time I had a breathing session, I didn't know what to expect. I struggled with the breathing pattern as it felt tight and painful in my chest. After a few sessions, I was able to breathe more fully and for longer periods. It helped with the mental aspect of training, giving me tranquillity and peace so I could focus on what was important, which was winning the fight and being in the best peak condition I could achieve.

I sensed that some people around me were rooting for me to fail. They preferred Bryan as the underdog. It made me feel paranoid, not knowing who to trust. The training is pretty vigorous and there is a lot of stress on my body physically, mentally and emotionally. It's intense.

The third breathing session was really powerful. I felt incredibly strong emotions resurfacing from my childhood, a period when I was hurt, and the anger I felt towards that memory was overwhelming. It was all coming through at once and really wanted to come out. I felt like I was being overtaken by a blind rage. I was the angriest I had ever been, but there was also fear and hurt.

I had to stop the session. I felt too embarrassed to continue and was also scared by the rage coming out of me. We talked it through and Rebecca assured me it was safe for us to do this. I just needed to give myself permission to let this go.

We went back into the breath session and a whole rush of emotion rose up and released itself in a torrent. Afterwards, I felt a lot clearer, like my brain had been to the gym. I also noticed that my relationship with my mum changed. The problem was still there, but I no longer hold any bad feelings about it. I have let it go. Getting upset with my dad about this stuff doesn't affect me the way it used to. I deal with it in a different way and can also better deal with people's attitudes and jealousy.

I've continued the breathwork in training, using affirmations for confidence, letting go of anxiety, and the two complement each other really well. It's still a work in progress, but it helps me in my relationship with myself as well as my relationships with others. I don't take things to heart so much now and have learned to let things go.

My granddad was a boxer and I can feel him watching over me. I recently won my title and it's given me the drive to go in a new direction, retire from competing and start my own gym training kids and adults.

I feel more peaceful, tranquil and in touch with my spiritual side, and I plan to bring that into my work. I really trust that it has helped me grow and look forward to where my path takes me next.

Conscious connected breath

Now that you have a deeper understanding of breath aware-ness and the benefits of breathing deeply into the belly, we can try a short conscious connected breath exercise. Please make sure that you have completed the other exercises first so that your breath is more aware of beginning in the belly, using the deep diaphragmatic breathing technique.

Reading the stories in this book, you will be aware that people have felt some sensations or emotions coming up dur-ing the exercises. I suggest we begin with a 2-minute exercise so as not to feel overwhelmed, and to fully understand the technique. Emotion doesn't always come up, but experience shows that mastering this technique first is best, and short sessions will help us achieve this. We spend so much time rushing in life and the aim here is to let that go. If at any point this feels too much for you, just come back to your normal breathing pattern and these feelings will pass.

It's always good to breathe through the sensations and trust your body. The important thing is not to control the breath. Eventually you will find that the breath becomes rhythmic, as if it is breathing effortlessly in a circular motion, coming in and out like a wave. It can take some time to get there, as with all practices.

It is important not to push or force out the exhale, as this may cause hyperventilation. This can happen when the breath is rushed. People often experience this when over-breathing in panic attacks for example.

⊨ EXERCISE ⊨

CONSCIOUS CONNECTED BREATH EXERCISE

Practise this for 1–2 minutes to begin with.

You can do this sitting up or lying down. If you are lying down, prop yourself up either with pillows or cushions at a semi-reclined angle. Make sure your neck is supported and you are warm and comfortable, bend your knees so your feet are flat on the floor. This will help the breath to come into the belly. Now place your hands on top of your belly (your lower abdominals) to help guide the breath there.

Let's set an intention for this exercise. Think about what you would like to let go of – perhaps something in your life that is holding you back. How would it make you feel if you could let it go, and what would it bring more of into your life? So, if you want to let go of negative thoughts and feel clearer, your intention could be 'clarity'.

Open the mouth wide and relax the jaw. Begin to breathe in and out of the mouth. Connect the breath so there is no pause in between the inhale and the exhale. A long, relaxed inhale and a soft exhale. Breathe into the belly. As you inhale, the belly rises, as you exhale the belly falls.

Your mouth may feel quite dry at first, but this feeling will pass the more you practise. Often the mind likes to distract us, when practising, by letting us think we are thirsty or need a drink. Remember that's a distraction.

The reason we are practising an open-mouth breath is to bring in more volume and flow.

The key is to emphasise the inhale and make it long and deep (about 3 times the length of the exhale).

Notice if you can feel any sensations in your body as you connect to the breath. The important thing is to breathe through them. If you feel an emotion coming up, breathe into it. Try not to analyse the emotion or the sensation and remain focused on the rhythm of the inhale and the exhale.

Imagine you are taking your first ever inhale, and then let the exhale go in a relaxed manner. As if you are misting a mirror with your breath – that's all the volume of the exhale you need. Not pushing it out, forcing it out or hanging on to it. Let it be a soft, gentle sigh.

Repeat this and connect the inhale with the exhale. There is no pause between the inhale and the exhale.

The breath becomes one continuous circular breath. This may feel quite hard at first and the mind might be saying: 'But I have made a long inhale, so I need to match the length with the exhale.' But the natural mechanism of the exhale is to just let go. Remember that connected pattern of a sleeping baby, a dog or a cat.

Come back to your normal breathing pattern and breathe in through the nose. Notice how you feel, perhaps more energised and buzzy, or calm and clear.

Finish with a big inhale through the nose, and let it go with a big sigh out of the mouth. Repeat this 3 times.

Some tips to help you achieve conscious connected breathing

Begin by grounding yourself. Get quiet. Feel the ground beneath your feet, push your heels and toes into the ground. Imagine roots coming out of your feet and into the ground.

Listen to the sounds around you. A clock ticking, birdsong, cars driving by, people chatting, the wind rustling the trees or rain falling.

Notice your breath and how it feels, and take a long, deep inhale and let the exhale go. In your mind say 'I' as you breathe in and 'let go' as you breathe out. Connect the breath, leaving no pause between the inhale and the exhale.

If your thoughts begin to wander, just regard them as clouds in the sky: the sky is always there but the clouds come and go, and allow the mind to drift back to the breath. It might be easier for you to count the breaths inside your head to keep focus.

Breathe into your tummy and allow the belly to rise and fall with each breath, recalibrating your system and resetting your thought processes with each breath.

Practise this for just a couple of minutes to begin with. If you begin to feel tingling or other sensations, breathe into this and through this. Remember to relax the exhale.

The more you practise, the more it will flow with ease. The key to all this is not giving up.

Meet a life-changer

I've met some magical people on this journey, who helped bring me back to myself and grow as a facilitator. One of them is Donna Lancaster. In her work she uses a variety of approaches, including rituals, to support people to release emotional blocks and return to who they really are.

Donna runs a programme called The Bridge, which is truly a life-changer. The combination of her work and breathwork is really powerful. I asked if she would contribute some words on grief. She very kindly agreed.

Donna Lancaster on grief

Grief is a natural reaction to any kind of loss. It is a normal and sometimes conflicting feeling usually associated with the death of someone we love – a partner, family member, friend or pet. However, there are many other life experiences that can produce grief:

Miscarriages/terminations

Moving house/location

Leaving a school/job

End of addictions

Major health changes/illness

Retirement

Financial changes

Empty nest

Loss of opportunities

Loss of trust/faith

Loss of identity from youth to middle age

Loss of innocence due to child abuse

Powerlessness

Grief is a fundamental part of the human condition. We grieve all of life's losses, not just bereavement. These endings are also a kind of death, bringing with them deep sorrows that require time and space to heal. Such 'deaths' involve losing aspects of ourselves, and they can happen not just a few times in our lifetime but monthly, weekly, even daily.

We experience loss many times in our lives, but most of us have been socialised to believe that expressing these feelings is abnormal or wrong in some way. Over time, the pain of unresolved grief is cumulative and can have a lifelong impact on a person's capacity for happiness. Depressive mood swings, hopelessness and anxious feelings are common reactions to unprocessed grief. I believe we need to honour these losses in the same way that we mark the gains in our lives, because both fundamentally change us. You could say that, just as we celebrate the 'comings' of life, such as an 18th birthday, marriage and childbirth, we also need to honour the 'goings'.

While we have the ritual of funerals to help us through the loss of friends and family, we are rarely taught how to honour and let go of other hurts, losses and betrayals in ways that are healthy for us. The result is that many of us store up these griefs, accumulating them year after year until, in our middle adult years, we find ourselves bursting with a pain so great that we cannot even contemplate examining it.

Instead, many of us simply batten down the hatches of our heart and endure. The result is that our life becomes smaller, shallower and narrower. Everything is less than it could be, including ourselves. This sense of 'less than' can mean not only that we lose our potential to thrive and make the most of our lives, but also that a coldness and bitterness of heart can set in.

This is the reason why many of us walk around in a cloud of negativity and indulge in moaning, bitching and gossip at work and at home. But I believe such negative behaviour is often a sign of unexpressed hurt, sadness and pain, which psychotherapist David Richo calls 'a poor man's grief'. The impact of this avoidance can be far-reaching.

In my work as a coach and facilitator of personal development programmes, I have worked with hundreds of people who describe themselves or have been diagnosed as 'depressed' or 'anxious'. And I have found again and again over the years that for many people this is a misdiagnosis, because what they are really suffering from is unprocessed grief.

Failure to process the impact of major life challenges can result in symptoms that look very similar to depression. This is not to deny that some people have clinical depression or anxiety disorders, but there are others who sense that they have been misdiagnosed, or who wrongly believe that they are depressives. In fact, they are suffering from a failure to turn and face specific issues of loss in their life that can be resolved and in the process save them from a life of pain and suffering.

But how to tell the difference? In my experience, if people are allowed a safe and nurturing space to express and make sense of blocked emotions arising from past hurts, betrayals and losses, what happens quite simply is that they get better.

Donna's top tips for dealing with loss

Honesty: Acknowledging to yourself and to trusted others the full range of feelings you are experiencing. It's important not to deny or ignore these feelings, nor to push them away with distraction activities such as comfort eating, alcohol, overworking or over-exercising. These diversions may provide short-term relief but they also delay the healing process and can extend the period of grieving.

Time and space: Allowing yourself the time and space to process your loss is key. Just as we stop and rest when we are sick, people need time to step out of their normal routine to allow the grieving process to flow. Of course it can feel easier to 'get busy' with an activity, but this does not allow the healing process to run its natural course. It is another kind of short-term 'fix' that prevents completion and moving on in the longer term. If possible, taking some time off work to do your 'grief work' can actually offer a faster and deeper route to recovering from the loss.

Allowing: Grief is essentially made up of three main feelings: sadness, anger and fear.
SADNESS – at what or who has gone away.
ANGER – at the unfairness, injustice, betrayal.
FEAR – that things will always feel/be this way.
It is important that you allow yourself to experience all of these feelings as they arise.

Expression: Write a letter to your lost one expressing all your hopes and dreams, sadness, fear and anger. This is a love letter from your heart to theirs, externalising your thoughts and feelings. It allows you to 'say the unbearable', including goodbye. Once written, it can be very healing to read this letter to a trusted friend who will simply listen. Being witnessed in this way validates your experience and is another step on your healing journey. Keeping a journal and sharing your changing experience of the loss through therapy can also be very supportive.

Body: Just as it is important to write and speak about your loss, it is also key to express the loss through the body. For many of us, a significant loss such as a miscarriage or bereavement can be experienced as a kind of trauma, which can get trapped in the body. Using the body and voice to trigger and safely release emotions can aid the healing process. Walking, dancing, breathwork, yoga, even bashing pillows all offer routes of expression through the body. Touch is also very supportive: being held, cuddled, someone holding your hand, having a massage. Never underestimate the healing power of touch.

Connection: Although this is often a time when people want to be alone, it is important to stay in connection with significant others. Spend time with family and friends, people who will allow you to simply be with your grief without trying to change it. A listening ear and a loving eye can make all the difference.

....

Our wounds are often the openings into the best and most beautiful part of us.

David Richo, psychotherapist and writer

....

Inner Child

Deep down inside all of us is our child self: playful, excited to explore and happy to be alive. As a child, we have the ability to imagine we are a superhero, a ninja-warrior princess or a helicopter pilot, flying through the sky, seeing other worlds and finding magic in everything. Every day is an adventure and the chance to learn something new, to wonder at the stars or look at the sea for the very first time. Our inner child still lives within us.

Often, when practising inner child work during sessions, we are able to access feelings and experiences from our child self that have either been blocked out or pushed down and suppressed as a way of protecting ourselves. When painful or uncomfortable events happen, our breath pattern changes and we relive the same old patterns, repeating behavioural and emotional reactions.

While breathwork is not about going into the story over and over again, but rather releasing it and living in the now, it can help us to reach a better understanding of how we can truly and authentically let it go. Each of us perceives and tells our story from our own perspective, and this perception can alter from one perspective to another. There is no right or wrong, and nothing is judged by the breath. Rather than judging, try simply to accept what it is.

Expectations

In his excellent book *Healing the Shame That Binds You*, John Bradshaw describes how the unacknowledged shame of the parent is passed down to the children. Take, for example, the mother whose only sense of accomplishment is felt through the behaviour and achievements of her children. Her own shame is transferred to the child whenever he fails to live up to her need for approval – she feels ashamed if he looks scruffy or misbehaves in front of his grandparents.

Expectations begin early in our lives. Maybe you feel under pressure to be someone, or wonder: 'Who am I?' The pressure we put on ourselves and each other to be something in society can make us feel inadequate if we don't think we've attained our target.

These questions and self-doubts start at a very early age. Recently, a client told me that she has been putting expectations on herself since the age of seven when she was first asked what she was going to be when she grew up. The child self in her has been constantly trying to prove herself ever since.

We don't mean to put expectations on others but it is ingrained in us to aspire to the perfect life, house, partner, promotion, car, pay rise, bigger house, bigger kitchen, another child.

The questions start young:

'What are you going to do when you're older?'

'What exams are you taking?'

'Are you going to university?'

'When are you going to find yourself a nice boyfriend or girlfriend?'

'When are you getting married?'

'So when are you going to have kids?'

Maybe you don't want a child and find yourself justifying your decision, or you haven't found the right person to have a child with yet. You feel as though others pity you. You might be having difficulty conceiving but feel the pressure from friends or members of your family who already have children. Women in this position tell me how exhausting it is keeping up a front and a smiling face every time they hear another friend is pregnant. Or perhaps their friend won't tell them they are pregnant because they don't want to upset them. It's an emotional minefield. If you have a child, will you be trying for another one? Don't you want another child?

STOP! Take a breath, please. You are perfect as you are. Love yourself as the precious thing you are. Because you are enough. Just as you are.

James, 35, is the owner of a successful restaurant chain.

James owns a successful restaurant chain with 250 employees. He loves his work and travels around the world presenting at conferences. He has a supportive and loving wife, three gorgeous children who are balanced, happy and doing well at school, and a great social life. Financially secure, he wouldn't need to work another day if he chose not to.

Out of the blue, he started experiencing major panic attacks. Usually very confident in meetings, James had to start cancelling them as the attacks left him feeling out of control. He was considering cancelling a big conference he was due to present at, as he had no idea what was triggering the attacks or when they might happen.

One day, he was driving with his daughter and experienced a panic attack. He had to pull over and felt very scared. On another occasion, it happened while he was with his son at a museum. He consulted doctors and panic attack specialists but nothing was working. His wife booked him in for a breathing session, feeling desperate to help him after he had a breakdown in front of her.

We spent half an hour going through his history before we began by practising the connected breath in his belly. His diaphragm was very tight and his breathing pattern showed he was an upper-chest breather with a lot of control issues. After a couple of sessions, he was able to bring the breath into his belly, and although the sessions were physically intense for him, resulting in a lot of tingling and numbness in his jaw, arms and hands, he was able to breathe through them.

James says: 'I realised that I hadn't dealt with a lot of stuff from my childhood. My father was a bully and my mother was an alcoholic. I'm ashamed to say that my father encouraged me and my brothers to be bullies, and told us that being vulnerable was a weakness.

'He is a ruthless businessman and I watched him ruin a lot of people's lives. My relationship with him now is very fragmented, and I have always tried not to be like him. I run a business where my employees are not ruled by fear, and I have striven to be a loving father to my children.

'There were some occurrences in my past that I had pushed down as a child, and I was able to go back and revisit them through my breath. I had no idea they had any relevance until now. It was very liberating to finally acknowledge them and let them go.

'I worry about my dad as I know that deep down he is an unhappy man, but I also know I can't change him. He has no desire to change. Part of me has been trying to prove myself to him for years. I realise that I was throwing myself into work as a part of me was unsure if I could ever be a loving and present father.

'As a result of the breathwork, my wife has noticed an enormous change in me and I spend a lot more time now with my children, being a present dad. I no longer have panic attacks and am enjoying being back at work.'

Making affirmations a reality

The philosophy of using positive affirmations is that while they may not feel true, with repetition they sink into your subconscious mind and eventually they become your reality. You don't have to say these affirmations out loud, but quietly in your head while connected to the rhythm of the inhale and the exhale. Using affirmations also stops us from wandering into our thoughts and keeps us focused on our intention.

In time, affirmations can overwrite any limiting beliefs you may have about yourself or about not being able to do something, and replace them with positive thoughts and beliefs which instil confidence, belief, positivity, ambition and much more.

⊨ EXERCISE ⊨

USING AFFIRMATIONS AND A CONSCIOUS CONNECTED BREATH

Practise this for 1 minute.

Create a comfortable space where you won't be interrupted, sitting or lying down. If you are lying down prop yourself up either with pillows or cushions at a semi-reclined angle as in the previous exercise and bend your knees with your feet flat on the floor. Close your eyes and take a deep breath. Feel the ground beneath you, connecting you to the Earth.

Imagine roots coming out of your feet and growing into the ground to help you feel centred.

Notice your breath and where the breath is in your body. How does it flow?

Breathe in through the mouth and out of the mouth, connecting the inhale and the exhale. Inhale deeply into your belly and just let the exhale go. Count in for 2 strokes on the inhale and 1 on the exhale. Remember, there's no need to push the river. The breath comes in and then just let it go. As you breathe in, the belly rises and as you breathe out, the belly goes down. Notice any pauses in between the inhale and the exhale. Allow the breath to become one continuous breath. Connect the inhale and exhale, with no pause.

Breathe in and use affirmations like the ones below, or make up your own.

'I am perfect as I am.'

'I am safe and welcome in this world.'

'I am enough.'

These are simply words we use to speak to the subconscious mind. We don't need to analyse it or think about what the words are referring to. Stay focused on the breath being connected.

Notice how the breath feels in your body. Is it in the belly, and is the breath connected?

Notice any feelings, emotions or sensations that come up as you breathe in and out, emphasising the inhale and softly letting the exhale go.

Now bring your breath back to its normal breathing pattern. Take a big breath in through the nose and let it go with a big sigh out of the mouth. Repeat 3 times.

When you feel comfortable and confident with this technique, move on to practising for longer, 3 minutes and then 4. Set a timer so that you don't need to look at a clock. If you feel any sensations coming up in the body, any tingling or emotion, breathe into it and through it. At no point do we want to push or force the exhale out. If it ever feels too overwhelming or intense, slow the breath down, try not to accelerate it, and come back to your normal breathing pattern.

Limitations are creations of the mind

In her brilliant book *Eastern Body, Western Mind*, Anodea
Judith explains:

> We match our behavior to our self-concept. Afraid of making
> mistakes, we dare not venture outward and keep ourselves
> small and limited, giving us just cause for our feelings of inferi-
> ority. Without the belief that we can succeed, we quit without
> really trying, and of course, in quitting, we prove to ourselves
> that we cannot succeed.

Facing our own truth

Ego punishes and judges us, love forgives and heals us. Yes, it
really is that simple.

All thoughts and words hold energy. This is why thoughts
and emotions get stronger the more attention we give
them. Let's say you feel a pang of jealousy or a little fear.
If you focus on it, it grows and becomes more infused with
energy.

Energy can pull us in. It happens with our children, at
work, with friends, strangers and loved ones. Letting go
means falling behind the energy. We tend to let ourselves get
bothered by meaningless things, such as a car aggressively
overtaking you. When these things happen, you will feel
your energy change.

To get back to your centre, try to relax your shoulders and

the area around your heart and breathe deeply and gently into your belly.

....

There's a place deep inside of you where the consciousness touches the energy, and the energy touches the consciousness. That's where your work is. From that place, you let go. Once you've let go, every minute of every day, year after year, then that's where you'll live. Nothing will be able to take your seat of consciousness from you. You'll learn to stay there. After you've put years and years into this process, and learned to let go no matter how deep the pain, you will achieve a great state. You will break the ultimate habit: the constant draw of the lower self. You will then be free to explore the nature and source of your true being – Pure Consciousness.

Michael A. Singer, *author of* The Untethered Soul

....

....

You either get bitter or you get better. It's that simple. You either take what has been dealt to you and allow it to make you a better person, or you allow it to tear you down. The choice does not belong to fate, it belongs to you.

Josh Shipp, *author and motivational speaker*

....

⊨ EXERCISE ⊨

I often use this meditation when processing or experiencing negative thoughts and energy. This meditation is adapted from Eugene Gendlin's focusing technique, which is a somatic method for fostering mindful self-awareness, allowing and acceptance.

Close your eyes, or focus on a spot on the floor, then begin to become aware of your breathing, placing your attention on the fact that you are breathing.

Notice that your breath is moving in and out, specifically as it enters and leaves the tips of your nostrils. Follow this breath from this point of focus, in and out, for a minimum of 10 cycles.

Allow yourself to sink into the 'just this-ness' of the breath flow. Simply notice the breath flowing in and out of your nostrils.

Do not adjust your breathing to be deeper or slower or faster, just allow it to flow in and out naturally.

Then allow your attention to locate the place in your body where you are most clearly experiencing painful thoughts and feelings about a recent event or something that has been weighing on your mind.

Often people feel sensations in their chest or belly area, but it can happen anywhere – just tune in to find yours. Then simply breathe and be with that place in your body.

Don't attempt to change it, but merely cradle that space with loving, kind awareness, breathing in and out, staying there for several breaths, and then return to the room and open your eyes. Thank yourself for paying loving, kind awareness and attention to yourself.

You can add an extra, more advanced facet to this meditation: while cradling the painful feeling in your body as described above, simultaneously expand your consciousness outward, first to the sounds in the room, then take your mind outward to the roof, the tops of the trees, and continue expanding and broadening your consciousness while continuing to return to and briefly touch into this pain in your body.

Bounce back and forth between expanded consciousness and acute pain.

When you are ready, return to the room and open your eyes.

Love Who You Are

Love is a state of Being. Your love is not outside; it is deep within you. You can never lose it, and it cannot leave you. It is not dependent on some other body, some external form.

Eckhart Tolle, author

Self-love

Some people feel uncomfortable talking about self-love, thinking that it sounds vain or boastful. I encourage people to love themselves all the time. The good parts and the not so good parts, the messy parts, the flawed parts, what we see and what we don't see.

When someone compliments you on how you look, do you reply with 'Oh, thank you', followed by a self-deprecating remark? It's not always easy to take compliments. We feel more at ease giving them than receiving them.

When it comes to silencing our inner critic, we need to let it know we are fine with not being good at everything. It's actually okay to fail. I had, and often still do have, the feeling of being a fraud, worrying that someone would catch me out at any minute. I'm willing to bet I'm not alone in that fear. Sometimes I wouldn't feel confident enough to speak up or explain a point so I'd choose not to say anything rather than say the wrong thing.

Some wise words from author J. K. Rowling: 'It is impossible to live without failing at something, unless you live so cautiously that you might as well have not lived at all – in which case, you fail by default.'

What I have learned, and am still learning, is that breathwork helps us to see and love the most real version of ourselves. We are always learning and growing; the journey never ends. Once you start digging, there's more digging to do.

By breathing consciously and acknowledging to ourselves that we are perfect as we are, imperfections and all, we value our whole self. We begin to treat ourselves and our minds the way a gardener treats their plants: pruning the blooms, pulling up weeds – our negative thoughts. We work from the roots, our subconscious, and dig the earth to make it nurturing for the plants to grow and thrive.

Passing it on

I believe that compassion, kindness, self-love and being a free spirit are the first qualities we should teach our kids. I work a lot with teenagers who struggle with self-esteem, often comparing themselves negatively to others. Sadly, body issues and competitiveness are rife, especially with social media freely accessible night and day.

We all want to be liked, to fit in at this emotionally vulnerable time of our lives. The social pressures on teenagers are relentless. Fashion magazines still glamorise size-0 models, and boys and girls aspire to that highly unrealistic and dangerous benchmark. Parents expect their children to perform to the highest levels, and children compare themselves to each other instead of supporting each other.

How can we teach our children to love themselves for who they are and allow them to flourish and develop their own unique individuality?

It is essential for children and teenagers to grow from their experiences – both negative and positive – and not shut themselves off from the world. Bullying is escalating and the levels of anxiety, stress, depression and suicide are also rising in this generation.

Society tends to demand the same level of academic success from all children, even though school achievement may not be a useful tool with which to evaluate their success in life.

Like flowers in the garden, children should be given the space to grow in their own unique way and be seen for their individual beauty with help and guidance from the wisdom of the gardener.

My clients impress me every day with their strength, and show me that this is warrior work. One young lady who really inspired me was Gaia.

Gaia, 16, is studying for her GCSEs. This is her story.

At the age of 5, I lost both my parents, my mother first, then my father. My mother suffered a head injury after a serious fall and later died in hospital. I didn't really understand what had really happened at that young age.

My father had cancer. He'd had his left arm amputated above the elbow to prevent it spreading, but unfortunately it was unsuccessful. I used to brush his hair and wonder why it fell out.

I moved in with my aunt – my mother's sister – but I never really settled. I always felt left out, so I asked to move to where I live now with my other aunt, my dad's sister. She has two grown-up daughters and they acted as sister role models for me.

About a year ago, I was told that my mother had been mentally ill and took drugs and drank. Everything suddenly made sense about how she used to act. I can recall times when I was about 3 and my mother would take me to the pub where she would get drunk. Once we left the pub and my mother was grabbed by a man and a woman and I was grabbed by another woman. I kicked and screamed, it was a terrifying experience.

All I can remember after that is being in a police station while my mother was taken away on a hospital bed with a mask over her face. Being told she was mentally ill finally made me realise why she behaved the way she did.

The news affected me quite a lot. I suffered from anxiety and would stress about things that would seem normal to anyone else. I feared that I was going to inherit her illness. A doctor labelled me anorexic, suicidal and depressed, and these labels started to define me in my medical records.

I had a long phase of being emotional, angry and suicidal, and adopted the same trend of self-harming as some of my friends. I managed to stop the self-harming last summer, but my GCSEs became a huge source of stress. My view was, if I didn't do well, I would never do well in life. Despite planning my school work and having guidance on revision, suicidal thoughts would flood my brain, haunting me day and night. I was constantly worrying about day-to-day life.

The turning point came when my cousin got me an appointment with Rebecca at a group session in London. When I first tried the technique, I felt like a complete idiot, bawling my eyes out in a room of 23 people. It wasn't until a man also cried that I felt comfortable and realised that we were all here for the same reason, to relieve, gain, or just to breathe and try this wonderful experience.

I continued to have private sessions with Rebecca and was able to talk and share everything I had been holding in. We would focus on key events that I had been through, and my problems became easier to see. The goal was to help me try to settle my past so that I could live life a bit more easily.

The breathwork is something I use every night to sleep better. I also use this method if I'm stressed or worried, and simply lie down and start to breathe the way I was taught to escape all my worries.

If it wasn't for breathwork, I don't know where I'd be. I'm finally back on my feet and making strong progress. Nothing seems like a challenge anymore.

Rose, 28, is a film producer. This is her story.

The way I dealt with low self-esteem, pain and feeling disconnected was to escape from myself. Eating disorders: tick. Drug habit: tick. Alcohol abuse: tick. Staying in abusive relationships: tick.

If I could meet my younger self now, I would give her an almighty great hug, because she really needed one. I would pick her up and teach her the best lesson in life: how to love herself.

I had a secret eating disorder for years. I always felt guilty around food, either hating myself for eating or hating myself for bingeing and bringing it back up again. I felt very ashamed and was caught in a vicious cycle of starving myself or making myself sick.

I was also getting out of my head to escape that feeling of disconnection, but most of all to escape from myself.

Breathwork rewired me to love and nurture myself. I began to eat more healthily because I loved my body and wanted to feed it well. Before, I just didn't care enough, and food was the one thing I felt I could control.

As I learned to love myself, I stopped craving a different life and ceased trying to escape from the one I was in. Thankfully, I could see that everything around me was inviting me to grow.

I learned to say no to what didn't feel right and started listening to what my heart wanted, freeing myself from what was not good for my wellbeing. It was simply a question of taking a breath, not living in the past or the future, but learning to live each day as it came.

I realised that my mind was a valuable ally, despite being a slightly annoying and destructive one at times. It was definitely no longer my master. I learned to trust my heart. I am still learning to accept confrontations, arguments and situations as part of life's rich tapestry. Most important of all, I learned to forgive myself.

⊨ EXERCISE ⊨

BREATHING INTO THE HEART

Feelings of guilt, shame and fear can hold us back from feeling joy, happiness and love in our heart. We can choose what feels best for us and fulfil our dreams and destiny only when we allow ourselves to trust the wisdom of our heart and let go of what the mind wants.

Whatever stories or thoughts have been holding you back and replaying over and over, give yourself permission now to let them go. Recognise that we are not our thoughts and that we have a choice.

Begin by setting an intention for what you would like to bring into your life.

Place one hand on your heart and the other on your belly.

As you inhale, the belly rises and as you exhale, the belly falls.

Remind yourself of your intention and continue to breathe in and out.

As you breathe into your heart, make the affirmations:

'I am true to myself. I love and accept myself.'

'I love and accept all parts of my being.'

Breathe in and out and notice as the mind tries to lead you back to your thoughts. Bring your mind back to your breath and breathe fully as you inhale, and give yourself permission to receive love and live life fully.

Breathe into your heart area and use the affirmations:

'I give myself permission to open my heart fully.'

'I love and accept every part of myself.'

Breathe into your heart and fill up your rib cage and belly with air as you breathe in and out.

As you breathe in, feel gratitude and love for the heart that beats for you every day and every night.

Now let the whole body release and let out the exhale with a big sigh.

With each breath, relax any tension, doubt or unkind feelings towards yourself. Tell yourself: 'I am perfect as I am.' Even if part of you doesn't believe this right now, in time you will.

Continue to connect with your breath, inhaling deeply and letting go as you exhale.

Intimacy

A deep awareness of our breath draws us closer to experiencing the power and vitality of all our senses.

In our hearts, we feel love, but we also experience shame,

guilt, fear, anger and grief. By letting go of these emotions, we are able to fully open our hearts and receive and express love. Emotional tension and fear of expression is often stored in the diaphragm. With the breath, not only are we exploring these feelings but we are also allowing them rather than hiding them away.

By letting go, we can transform fear into excitement. Many of us lack self-esteem, and breathwork helps us to be confident in our sexuality and truly love ourselves, even the parts that we don't particularly like. Some are deep-rooted and buried in our subconscious, but through the breath, we track them, hold them and release them in a gentle, non-invasive way.

Breathing free of tension brings us into the full awareness of ourselves and allows us to experience our true loving nature, offering us the tools to express intimacy through body and mind. With practice and understanding, we engage in a deep connection with ourselves and learn to accept all our feelings. Expressing our vulnerabilities is the foundation of deep intimacy with ourselves and with others.

One of the groups I work with, Shh . . . (sensualhealing-harmony.com), runs retreats for women. The results we see in the women who attend are always beautiful and moving. It's wonderful for women to get together in this way, empowering each other from the foundation that we all have the same insecurities. I work often with Shh . . .'s Sarah Rose Bright, and am thrilled to include her contribution below, as well as an exercise for you to work with.

Sarah Rose Bright, tantra coach.

Over a decade ago, I hated my body and how I looked. I was constantly comparing myself to others, telling myself what I was not. My self-criticism was endless, debilitating, and affected my confidence in all aspects of my life, including sex. Admitting this and doing something about it was one of the most challenging things I have ever undertaken, but also the most liberating and transformative.

A decade on, I now work as a sex and pleasure coach, and many of the people I work with have body image issues.

The quality of your relationship with yourself influences the quality of your relationship with everyone else. To really see, accept and love our true selves requires intimacy with ourselves before we can be truly intimate with another. Our bodies are our bridge, our interface with the world, and how we feel about them affects everything.

However, modern life does not support our cultivating a healthy relationship with our bodies. We live in a very disembodied world, learning mainly through our brains rather than our beings. Our bodies are treated like machines that need fuel and fixing when 'broken' rather than living organisms that need sensitivity and nurturing.

We live in a culture that sends strong messages that we're not good enough as we are. It promotes perfectionism and perpetuates comparison with what we don't have and what we lack. At extremes, this can result in self-loathing manifesting in addictions, self-harm and eating disorders.

There are a myriad of different reasons why people shallow

breathe. Abuse, trauma, childbirth, ageing and illness all have a significant impact on how we feel about our bodies and our ability to be present in them. For many people, sadly the body has not felt like a safe place to be.

So how do we come home to our bodies and learn to honour and love them for the amazing miracles they are? How do we learn to nourish and nurture them, accept and celebrate them?

The first stage is absolutely the breath. If you are not breathing fully, everything else will have limited impact. To breathe correctly means to optimise the health and vitality of our bodies. I work with all my clients on their breathing, and for many this alone is very powerful. Often clients immediately notice benefits such as feeling calmer, sleeping better and experiencing less stress. Sexual problems start to reduce too, and the quality of sexual pleasure changes.

The breath is a gateway to feeling more fully and being more present in the here and now, rather than being prisoners of our minds, worrying about the past or future, or exposing ourselves to constant self-criticism and comparison.

══ EXERCISE ══

SARAH'S MIRROR EXERCISE

Mirror work is very powerful. It is where we meet our inner selves and remember who we truly are when we are not judging ourselves. A place where we can start to find compassion, the magic elixir and key to the door of self-love.

This exercise is most effective when it is practised daily (it only takes a few minutes). It is an ongoing practice to learn to love your body. I've been doing this for over 10 years, and it works.

Imagine your mind and body as a garden. Negative thoughts are like weeds that you need to keep clearing so they don't take over the garden. You need to keep sowing seeds that turn into beautiful flowers, tending them with water and love so that they blossom. With this practice, every day you are tending your garden and bringing more and more beauty to your life.

Stand in front of a full-length mirror where you won't be disturbed for 5 minutes. You can do this fully or partially clothed or naked, whatever feels comfortable. Close your eyes and take a few deep breaths.

Open your eyes, and rather than immediately looking into the mirror and starting to judge and criticise what you see, allow your eyes to softly receive the image of yourself, breathing as you do.

Notice how this feels. Does it feel different? In what way?

Do you feel tense, uncomfortable, curious or relaxed? There is no right or wrong, you are just witnessing your feelings.

If an inner conversation starts, take your attention back to your breathing. Your breath is an anchor out of the mind and into the here and now.

I'm inviting you to find 3 things that you appreciate, like or love about your body. For example, 'I like my hair.' Say this silently or out loud, and as you do, breathe and allow these words to travel through the whole of you. In the same way that you ingest food, ingest these words.

It may be your eyes, the shape of your body or your skin. You choose! If you struggle with that (and many do), then find things you appreciate, perhaps 'I appreciate my breath for keeping me alive', or 'I appreciate my heart for pumping the blood around my body.'

Some days, you may find yourself repeating what you appreciate, like or love. That's totally fine, as you are reprogramming your thoughts and focusing on what you value rather than criticising and comparing yourself.

This exercise may feel uncomfortable and awkward but there is much truth in the old adage 'Fake it till you make it.' This is a process, and some days will be easier than others. The key is to keep showing up and doing this. It gets easier over time, I promise.

You may find that you feel sad as you become more aware of how you speak to yourself. The Ho'oponopono prayer is an ancient Hawaiian practice of forgiveness. You recite: 'I'm sorry, I love you, please forgive me, thank you.' Forgiving ourselves is the hardest thing of all. Ho'oponopono is transformative and creates space for us to heal and move forward rather than get trapped in negative emotions.

At the end, look into your eyes and say your name followed by 'I love you.' If this is too much, try 'I am learning to love you.' As you say this, smile with love and appreciation for your courage.

Breathing with Nature

....

Nature does not hurry, yet everything is accomplished.

Lao Tzu, philosopher

....

The Earth is our medicine

Have you ever been so enchanted or caught up that time just seems to disappear? Have you been mesmerised by the moon or the heart of a flower and its delicate details? Have you seen a cobweb sprinkled with dew, sparkling like tiny diamonds, and it feels like no one else has noticed it except you? Being in the presence of a deer deep in the forest and watching her, unaware of you as she ambles through the trees. Watching the sun set over a beautiful horizon. A whale teaching her newborn how to breach in the deep blue sea, or a humming-bird taking nectar from a flower. A snake skimming past you on the sand.

At times like this, when we marvel at the beauty of the world and all the gifts that Mother Nature presents to us, we are enchanted by the impeccable systems of the Earth that have been bestowed on us. No one can really explain how we got here, but we can all agree on one thing: being alive on this wonderful planet is truly miraculous.

The wonders of the world are not always this obvious to us, however, and we can easily become disillusioned by what is happening in our lives and in the outside world.

We live in a world where thousands of parentless children roam the streets trying to escape war. Our governments give corporations permission to destroy the land and natural habitat of the animals and tribes who have lived there for thousands of years. Forests are being flattened and replaced by vast farming conglomerates and oil companies. And the trees, plants, marine plants and algae that give us the very oxygen we need to breathe are treated with little respect or gratitude.

In short, people are becoming more and more disconnected from the Earth that we live in.

Imagine a world where there are no borders or control, no war, where fear and hate are replaced by love and acceptance. Where the waters are not polluted and the trees, plants and animals are respected and honoured by everyone for their part in the working systems on this planet.

Perhaps it sounds impossible. Indeed, many people choose to live their lives ignoring what is happening around them and what part they could play, while others passionately campaign and protest to protect our Earth and humanity. Some seek to effect the change while others simply freeze and feel dismayed and helpless.

But if human beings created all this chaos in the first place, and if we are as intelligent as we like to think we are, surely we can reverse this, reconnect, and collectively take responsibility to begin to reverse the damage that we have caused.

Connecting to nature around us – the forests, magical landscapes and elements – inspires us. As my little boy says, 'Everything is alive in the woods.' He's right: he can feel it and so can I. The trees are alive, the great yew tree, the ancient oak, they are living beings. It's not just our imagination playing fantastical games.

The world is so rich in its bountifulness and beauty, showering us with gifts. Allow yourself to receive all of this and spend time in nature. Whenever you feel overwhelmed or don't know what to do next, simply take yourself off to sit under your favourite tree. Stay still and rather than think, just breathe and wait. Listen for the answer and it will come.

Forest bathing

People all over the world understand the restorative power of being around and connecting to nature. Forest bathing is popular in Japan. Qing Li, president of the Japanese Society of Forest Medicine, has conducted a number of experiments to test the effects of forest bathing – or what we might call a walk in the park or forest – on our moods, stress levels and immune systems.

In one study, the Profile of Mood States test was used to show that forest bathing trips significantly increased the score of vigour and decreased the scores for anxiety, depression and anger, leading to the recommendation that habitual forest bathing may help to decrease the risk of psychosocial stress-related diseases.

I have a great love and respect for trees. I even called my company Breathing Tree. I am lucky to live in a home surrounded by woodland where I can sit with trees and listen to their wisdom whenever I choose. But I never take that for granted. Trees are part of the system that helps us to breathe. A mature leafy tree produces as much oxygen in a season as 10 people inhale in a year, and the forest acts as a giant filter that cleans the air we breathe. Isn't nature incredible?

⊨ EXERCISE ⊨

WALKING MEDITATION EXERCISE

Practise this with a soft breath and an open heart.

Take a walk somewhere natural (if you live in a city, head to your favourite park).

Before you begin, stand still, take a pause, and put the rest of the day behind you. This time and space is for you. Turn off your phone.

Feel the ground beneath you, take a few deep breaths, and become aware of your breath and notice where it is.

Find a balance, find your centre, and practise being rather than doing, accepting the breath where it is today.

As you walk at a normal pace, connect to your breath and take note of this constant companion that is with you throughout the day, feeling the rise and fall of the breath coming in and out.

As you place one foot onto the ground and the next foot in front of it, notice how your feet feel and the change in balance as the body moves through space. Feel your constant connection to the ground with each step, allowing your arms to move freely, and become aware of the sights and sounds around you.

Be here now in this moment with each step, and each time the mind wanders, guide it back to the sensation of your feet on the ground, lifting, stepping, placing. Stay in the present moment.

What colours and textures do you see? Have you spotted something you haven't noticed before?

Take a few deep breaths and continue to walk at a gentle pace.

Take your attention to the sounds around you: what do you hear? Focus on the sounds closest to you. Can you hear your feet crunching on the ground beneath you, traffic close by, the sound of people or birds?

Keep your attention on your breath and on the soles of your feet as you continue to move, and notice the rhythm of your breath matching, and feeling peace and tranquillity with each step.

Coming Home

We all follow patterns, whether we are aware of it or not. What I learned through breathwork is how to track my patterns and let the unhealthy ones go. It's incredibly empowering.

I now know where my home is. It's inside me. I've had a good sort-out, swept away a lot of cobwebs and confronted the skeletons in my closet. The breath helped me to have an emotional spring clean. Every time we practise this work, we are decluttering and dispelling the things that are no longer required, to create a space that we can call home.

Breathing through depression

I can't explain why depression chose me. It doesn't discriminate: it's not about whether you are a good or bad person, what colour or gender you are, if you're rich or poor.

If you are reading this and have experienced depression, you'll know how hard it is to explain to people how it feels when the cloud comes over you. With me, it would usually descend every three to six months. One minute I'd be happily plodding along and then BAM, it would hit me like a hammer and floor me for no particular reason. I can identify some triggers at certain points in my life, but there was no real rhyme or reason; it didn't choose the hard times in life, it just came whenever it pleased.

Depression would make me forget who I was. It would disconnect me from the world. Many of us have no idea who to talk to or how to get through it. When you are feeling sad, lethargic and uninterested in life, it's nigh on impossible to know where to start, but breathing consciously gave me hope and helped me to feel steady in my inner world again.

Incredibly, 1 in 4 people live with this illness, and many suffer in silence. But thankfully, the taboo is starting to lift, and people are beginning to speak out about it and seek new ways to treat it. Medical science and research is evolving constantly, and there is a wealth of information for people to access.

As you know, I was lucky to feel supported enough to come off my medication after 15 years, which took courage. On the rare occasions that I feel a grey cloud looming, I work with my breath and other tools. I hope that more people can be empowered to do the same.

Please always consult your doctor if you want to try and come off your medication, and remember there is absolutely no shame in being on medication if it is working for you. If you are struggling with your moods, go and see a doctor, as they are there to help. Mindfulness, yoga and breathing techniques will continue to be useful allies either way.

In one breath session during my training, I accessed

the part of me that didn't want to be here on this Earth. It was one of the most profound breathing sessions I have ever had. It was heartbreaking and beautiful at the same time, and it showed me why I have been given this life and the best way for me to go forward and embrace it fully.

As Judith Kravitz says:

The more we experience our own clear connection with Higher Power, Spirit, Universal Consciousness – or whatever name you prefer in referring to the Divine – the more faith we develop in ourselves and in life itself. True faith leads to true peace, and because faith is the realisation that it's all good, all of life is a gift and a blessing.

Feeling at home in your foundations

A lot of people bandy around the word 'grounded'. They talk of 'being grounded' or 'wanting to ground myself', but many of us don't really understand what this means.

We are energetic beings, and like the electricity in our homes we need to be earthed. Think of it as if you are plugging yourself into the Earth's energy. This gives us the solid foundation we need to feel secure and stable and allows the energy to flow through us more freely.

When we feel firm and secure in our foundations, it is easier for us to move through any blockages or obstacles. So whenever you can, take your shoes off, walk barefoot and feel that connection with the Earth that gives us the foundations to walk and live on.

BREATHING MEDITATION TO GROUND US WITH THE ELEMENTS

Take yourself inwards and feel your sitting bones on the floor. Imagine that you have roots coming out of the base of your spine and they are growing into the ground, connecting you to the Earth. Earth, air, water and fire are around us and in all of us.

Take a deep breath in and a deep breath out, feeling the connection with the ground beneath you.

As you breathe in, feel the energy of the Earth coming up and through you.

Breathe in and breathe out.

Connect to the fire within you that burns deep inside, keeping the sparks of life alive.

Imagine the sun on your skin and on the top of your head and breathe in and out as you feel the sun's warmth all over your body.

Connect to the water inside you, your blood that carries nutrients to your cells, and connect to the water around you that keeps you cleansed and hydrated.

Breathe in and breathe out.

Connect to the air we breathe from outside to inside and

breathe in, giving thanks to the air that keeps us alive.

Take a deep inhale from the base of your spine all the way to the top of your head and breathe out.

Sound and Vibrations

In my 20s, I was looking after artists for a management company. One of them was the legendary harmonica player Larry Adler. Larry had so many amazing stories about Hollywood . . . he'd played tennis with Charlie Chaplin and Greta Garbo, hung out with Al Capone, had a love affair with Ingrid Bergman, and enjoyed a long-standing friendship with the Gershwin brothers.

George Gershwin, who wrote 'Summertime', told Larry after he played *Rhapsody in Blue*, 'The goddamn thing sounds as if I wrote it for you.'

We travelled the world together on tour with other artists and orchestras. Beatles producer Sir George Martin produced one of Larry's albums, and I can personally attest to the fact that every musician he asked to collaborate with him agreed without a second thought.

Larry was 80 years old and I was 22. We would get some funny looks as we boarded a plane or checked into a hotel, with people trying to work out our relationship. I didn't care. I loved that man.

Larry taught me about musicians and how they worked with their breath. He'd say: 'You need to inhale on the C and exhale on the F.' He certainly knew how to work with his breath and use his full lung capacity. Every breath made a sound. Larry even escaped from hospital when he was very ill in the last few months of his life, to play one last concert at the Royal Albert Hall.

Working with this legend was a divine gift to experience music in its finest, most intimate form. Each note he played would touch my heart. Every night, he stepped onto the stage to rapturous applause, and then silence would fall and he would play the first note. I would never fail to shed a tear; I guess it was gratitude for simply being in the moment. I always acknowledged how special that was.

It was the same pieces night after night, with a different artist or orchestra, and each time he played them, somehow there were different sounds and different emotions. He could read the audience and knew how to play them. Larry always said that anyone can play the harmonica, but only a true musician can make it sound musical.

Sound is a harmonic healer

Music moves us, it carries us through emotions, taking us back in time to different states of consciousness, raising our vibrations and bringing us into a higher vibrational state. When working with sound and music in sessions, it's as though there is another therapist in the room.

Music guides and encourages the breath to find its rhythm, move away from the mind, expand our awareness inside, nourishing our cells. The vibrations of certain sounds can help to bring us back to feelings of harmony, joy and wellbeing. Wave forms and frequencies permeate everything, including our thoughts and emotions.

I asked my dear friend Jess to contribute a simple sound meditation. The universe brought me and Jess together way back in my hazy advertising days, and we have been on many adventures and have remained the best of friends ever since.

⊨ EXERCISE ⊨

SIMPLE SOUND MEDITATION BY JESS HORN, CERTIFIED ISHTA YOGA TEACHER

As we are energy and vibrational beings, it makes perfect sense that sound vibrates in different parts of our body. Music speaks to your soul and can bring you to tears or uplift your mood instantly.

Yogis have known about the power of sound for thousands of years, and there is a whole branch of yoga devoted to sound: mantra yoga.

We are going to play with making some sound with an exercise adapted from an ISHTA yoga meditation.

OM or AUM, probably the most well known of all Sanskrit syllables, is used by people all over the world to begin and end their yoga practice. So what does it mean?

It's said to be the primary sound of the universe, the sound that contains all sounds.

We are going to break down the A-U-M into four parts:

Chanting the:

Ahhh – and feeling it in the base of the spine. This is related to the unconscious.

Ohhh – and feeling it in the heart and throat. This is related to the subconscious.

Mmmm – and feeling it in the face and skull. This is related to consciousness.

And most importantly, the fourth part . . .

The silence – and feeling it in the crown of the head. This is related to super-consciousness and a connection with the universe.

Find a comfortable seat, somewhere you won't be disturbed.

Close your eyes and begin to notice your breath, the simple ebb and flow of the inhale and exhale.

Take a deep inhale and place your hands on your lower belly.

Sound Ahhh 3 times, feeling the vibration at the bottom of your spine and pelvic area.

Rest in silence for a couple of breaths.

Take a deep inhale and place your hands on your heart area.

Sound Ohhhh 3 times, feeling the vibration at your heart and throat.

Rest in silence for a couple of breaths.

Sound Mmmm 3 times, feeling the vibration in your head.

Rest in silence for a couple of breaths.

Then put it all together, sounding the A, the U and the M and feeling the power of the vibration in the silence.

Take a deep inhale and allow the A-U-M to combine into AUM, feeling the vibrations move through the body. Do this 3 times.

After the 3 AUMs, rest in silence for a couple of minutes. Notice the effects of the vibration upon your mind and body.

This is a lovely way to enter into meditation and connect to our inner vibration.

Inspiration

Take courage

Be inspired. Release your creativity. There are plenty of reasons why we don't engage with our wild, creative side and they are usually based in fear.

Think about your aspirations, your dreams, and find the strength and courage inside you to ignite your magic. We know what will happen if you don't. That's right, nothing.

Who knows what will happen if you do? That's the exhilarating part.

Maybe you want to write a book, learn to play an instrument, hone a new skill, climb a mountain, sing in a band, dance the salsa, go skinny dipping in a river, spend a night under the stars, travel the world, go on an adventure, be an artist. There may be all sorts of things you wish you had pursued, and maybe you feel like you are too self-conscious, too old to go for it.

Believe me when I tell you it's never too late. Take yourself on an inward journey with your breath and ask what makes your heart sing.

What are you afraid of? Face your fears and demons – they

are never as scary as you think they are going to be. Be brave, have courage, and be the warrior you always have been.

If you ever met me, you wouldn't look at me and think, 'Oh, she's got it all worked out.' Because I haven't! I am a work in progress, but every day I am inspired by the breath, the people who are pioneering this work, and my greatest teachers, my clients.

Do I still get angry? Yes. Do I still get scared? Of course. Do I mess up? Indeed. Do I still feel nerves when I speak in groups? Absolutely, because I am a human being and I will always have my flaws.

But I see the world through a very different filter now. I wake up in the morning and feel excited about what the day will bring. I feel a greater connection to Source, the divine, whatever you want to call it. In the course of writing this book, quite a few challenges came my way but I didn't let them stop me in my tracks as they might have done before. I used my anchor, my breath.

Life happens, good and bad things happen. Embrace the light and the dark. Always. We have to learn how to be part of the dance, and if we stumble, just make it a feature of the dance. On a spiritual level, there is no good or bad, there is only energy.

The way forward

How can we help the next generation? By teaching them about the fundamental gifts in life that nature has granted us, how to breathe consciously, not to judge and instead to accept everyone for who they are with compassion. Wouldn't it be good to know when we leave this Earth that we have done everything in our power to raise consciousness, so that the next generation can continue to breathe the air that we have been blessed to breathe and have access to the wonders of this planet? Look at this world as though through a child's eyes for the first time. Never forget how amazing it is.

Warrior vs Superman

Be that Zen warrior whose breath begins deeply from the belly, and not Superman, with the puffed-out chest. Everything is within you: a warrior does not give up. True courage is absolute vulnerability. Many of us feel lost in this world because of the fading state of our connection to our spiritual nature. Imagine what our lives would be like if we had never lost that connection to our spirit.

Be inspired. Be the change. Many of the old systems are no longer working; they are grinding to a standstill. Governments are crumbling, people are listening less to what the media says and choosing to find out and share information themselves. We can either sit in front of our TVs and vote for our children's future like it's *The X Factor*, or we can believe that we have a voice that can be heard and make a difference to the world we live in.

Don't be led by fear, it's a very old and negative pattern. We have access to so much information and we can choose to ignore it or embrace it and act NOW. We are all human beings living on this Earth together, so let's inspire each other to make this world a more peaceful, loving and compassionate planet. We are a tiny part of this universe, yet we are the universe, and how we act, react and choose to live affects everyone and everything on a global level.

This is a scary yet exciting time and finally, people are waking up. The time is now. Breathe. Let life breathe the way it wants to. Let yourself be free of conflict and tension. We all breathe the same air. We all have the capabilities to create peace on this Earth, and together we can achieve this.

Remember, your breath is always there, always listening . . . You just have to breathe.

⊨ EXERCISE ⊨

A LITTLE BREATHING MEDITATION TO FEEL INSPIRED

Close your eyes and take a few deep breaths. Your energy field is formless and knows no bounds.

Now begin to breathe with the following intention:

Breathe in light. Breathe out light.

Breathe in love. Breathe out love.

Breathe in peace. Breathe out peace.

Surrender to your breath and how you are feeling right now.

Allow the breath to guide you and show the way.

Allow breath to open your heart.

Allow breath to take you to a space inside.
Feel the breath inside you.
Relax and let go with each inhale.
Feel your own inner rhythm.
Surrender and trust that the breath is right.
Where does your breath want to take you today?

Some Simple Exercises for Every Day

You don't always need a plan. Sometimes you just need to breathe. Close your eyes, connect to your heart, and listen only to the sound of your breath for a full 5 minutes. Breathe in, breathe out. Let go. Your soul will thank you.

⊨ EXERCISE ⊨

EXPANDING YOUR CREATIVITY

Put one hand on your heart and one hand on your belly.

As you breathe quietly, notice how comforting that feels.

Be aware that you can do this anytime and anywhere.

Let your heart open and make room for all the good of the universe to come in.

As you breathe in, feel yourself allowing the creativity to flow.

As you breathe out, let go of any self-doubt or inner judgement.

As you breathe in, feel the breath and the energy coming all the way down into your feet.

As you breathe out, let go of the outside and continue to travel inwards.

Feel in the body any areas that are trying to hold on, and allow the breath to move its own way.

You may notice your thoughts coming in and out. Without judgement, observe those thoughts. Don't push them away, just observe them.

Stay focused on the breath and surrender to it.

When we connect our breathing, we connect to our inner wisdom.

Keep connected to this feeling as you go through your day, onwards and inwards.

BALANCING BREATH FOR CENTRING YOURSELF

If right-handed, place the thumb of your right hand over the right nostril and exhale through the left nostril.

Breathe into the left nostril to the count of 8 and hold the breath to the count of 8.

Cover the left nostril with the index finger of the right hand and exhale through the right nostril to a count of 8 and hold the breath for a count of 8.

Cover the right nostril with the thumb and repeat the cycle 10 times.

(If left-handed then simply reverse instructions of right and left.)

'HA BREATH' FOR DIGESTION AND JOYFUL ENERGY

Stand with the feet placed shoulder width apart with knees bent.

Place your hands on your lower abdomen and inhale through the mouth, expanding the diaphragm.

Exhale quickly through the mouth making the sound 'ha'.

Repeat rapidly for 2 minutes.

CAN'T SLEEP? TRY THIS SIMPLE 4-7-8 EXERCISE

This little exercise helps you to connect with your body and your breathing, distracting you from everyday thoughts that may keep you awake at night. It helps to relax and rebalance the nervous system, which can become overstimulated during stress, and promotes a state of calm.

Exhale completely through your mouth, making a 'whoosh' sound.

Close your mouth and inhale quietly through your nose to a mental count of 4.

Hold your breath for a count of 7.

Exhale completely through your mouth, making a 'whoosh' sound, to a count of 8.

This is 1 breath. Now inhale again and repeat the cycle 3 more times for a total of 4 breaths.

KUNDALINI BREATH FOR PHYSICAL ENERGY

Stand with feet placed shoulder width apart with knees bent.

Raise both arms above your head as you inhale through the mouth.

Quickly exhale through the mouth as you bring the arms down to shoulder height.

Inhale immediately as you raise the arms. Repeat for 2 minutes at a moderate pace to begin with, increasing time and intensity as you progress.

References and Resources

William Walker Atkinson, *Science of Breath*

Dr Elizabeth Blackburn and Dr Elissa Epel, *The Telomere Effect*

John Bradshaw, *Healing the Shame That Binds You*

Michael Brown, *The Presence Process*

Richard P. Brown, MD, and Patricia L. Gerbarg, MD, *The Healing Power of the Breath*

Deepak Chopra, *Ageless Body, Timeless Mind*

Donna Farhi, *The Breathing Book*

Ana Forrest, *Fierce Medicine*

Thich Nhat Hanh, *Anger*

Sandra Ingerman, *How to Heal Toxic Thoughts*

Anodea Judith, *Eastern Body, Western Mind*

Liz Koch, *Core Awareness*

Judith Kravitz, *Breathe Deeply, Laugh Loudly*

Al Lee and Don Campbell, *Perfect Breathing*

Peter A. Levine, *In an Unspoken Voice*

Dr Candace Pert, *Everything You Need to Know to Feel Go(o)d*

Swami Rama, Rudolph Ballentine, MD, and Alan Hymes, MD, *Science of Breath*

Michael A. Singer, *The Untethered Soul*

Jo Ann Staugaard-Jones, *The Vital Psoas Muscle*

Eckhart Tolle, *The Power of Now*

Music for breathing sessions
Tina Malia & Shimshai, 'Gayatri Mantra'
Craig Pruess & Ananda, 'Devi Prayer'
Buddha Bar, *Buddha Bar Nature*
Xavier Rudd, *Spirit Bird*

How to find facilitators for breathing one-on-ones, workshops and retreats
www.breathingtree.co.uk
www.inspirationspace.co.uk
www.transformationalbreath.com
www.transformationalbreath.co.uk

Acknowledgements

Deepest gratitude to all who have supported me on this journey. Thank you to my publisher Amanda Harris for asking me to write this book, and to all at Orion. Blessings and thanks to my wonderful agent and friend Valeria Huerta, my family, clients and teachers. Special thanks from the depths of my heart to Karen Hockney, thank you so much Jessie Horn and Aimee Hartley for holding the fort, keeping me sane, making me laugh always and cheering me all the way, I love you both so much. Thank you to my beautiful, brave sister Sarah for believing that I could do this and all your encouragement. Thank you to my mum and Ruthie, to Judith Kravitz and Steven Gooby for your wisdom and guidance and all the Breath family. Russell Storey, Pippa Wheble, Alan Purves, Donna Lancaster, Sarah Rose Bright, Thao Dang, Ronica Joshi, Kristi Mae Rodelli, Alan Dolan. Thanks to my wonderful friend Sarah Owen – aka Bunty.

Special thanks to all my amazing clients who contributed their stories and inspire and teach me every day.

Thank you to Georgie and everyone at Indaba; to my wifeys Di Redvers and Jo Parsons; to Jamie Grant, and all my beautiful friends. Wasinga family, you guys rock, the world always seems a better place with you. To Wendy Mandy,

Denis Whyte and all the other wizards and wizardesses in my life. Last but by no means least, to my husband Tom and my beautiful son Louis, who teaches me every day.

Credits

The author and publisher would like to thank the following copyright-holders for permission to reproduce extracts on the following pages:

26 *Breathing: The Master Key to Self-Healing*, Andrew Weil, audio book published by Sounds True, 15 November, 1999

26 *Perfect Breathing: Transform Your Life One Breath at a Time*, Al Lee and Don Campbell

31 *Mapping Emotions On The Body: Love Makes Us Warm All Over*, Lauri Nummenmaa, published on www.NPR.org

34 *The Miracle of Mindfulness*, Thich Nhat Hanh, published by Rider Books, Penguin Random House, UK

35 TEDx Talk, Max Strom

38 *The Collected Works, Volume Eight*, C. G. Jung, published by Routledge, Taylor & Francis

46, 56 *The Breathing Book*, Donna Farhi, published by Owl Books, Henry Holt

70 *Longstreet* (Paramount, 1971)

97 *The English Library*, Lao Tzu, published by Penguin Random House

100 *How to Heal Toxic Thoughts*, Sandra Ingerman, published by Sterling

111 *A Life Worth Breathing*, Max Strom, published by Skyhorse, 2010

114 Thich Nhat Hanh, Twitter, 2014

115 Dr Philippa Wheble

119 *Core Awareness*, Liz Koch, published by North Atlantic Books

120 *The Vital Psoas Muscle*, Jo Ann Staugaard-Jones, published by Lotus Publishing

123 TEDx Talk, Amit Soot

123 *Ageless Body, Timeless Mind*, Deepak Chopra, published by Rider Books, Penguin Random House, UK

140 *The Power of Coincidence*, David Richo, published by Shambhala, 1998

149 *The Untethered Soul*, Michael A Singer, published by New Harbinger, 2007

152 *The Power of Now*, Eckhart Tolle, published by Namaste Publishing, 1999